## More praise for *Fearless Career Change*

"*Fearless Career Change* promises to be the performance of your life-time!"

—Sharon K. Thorpe, Associate Director, Career Center,
University of North Carolina at Charlotte

"A great resource for all students and alumni. A viable tool in assessing interests, skills, and values."

—Veda Swift Jeffries, Assistant Director Career
Development Center, Stanford University

"Marky Stein's book *Fearless Career Change* is a clear workbook for a happier career. It might help you to find a better career, a reward-ing job, and a fuller life."

—Lyle Troxell, host of Geek Speak, KUSP Radio,
an NPR station, http://geekspeak.org/

# FEARLESS
# CAREER
# CHANGE

# FEARLESS CAREER CHANGE

## The Fast Track to Success in a New Field

## Marky Stein

### McGraw-Hill

New York   Chicago   San Francisco
Lisbon   London   Madrid   Mexico City
Milan   New Delhi   San Juan   Seoul
Singapore   Sydney   Toronto

1 2 3 4 5 6 7 8 9 0   AGM/AGM   0 9 8 7 6 5 4

ISBN 0-07-143912-9

McGraw-Hill books are available at special quantity discounts to use as premiums and sales promotions, or for use in corporate training programs. For more information, please write to the Director of Special Sales, McGraw-Hill Professional, Two Penn Plaza, New York, NY 10121-2298. Or contact your local bookstore.

 This book is printed on recycled, acid-free paper containing a minimum of 50% recycled, de-inked fiber.

**Library of Congress Cataloging-in-Publication Data**

Stein, Marky.
    Fearless career change : the fast track to success in a new field  /  Marky Stein.
       p.  cm.
    Includes index.
    ISBN  0-07-143912-9 (alk. paper)
    1. Career changes.   I. Title.
HF5384.S74   2005
650.1—dc22

2004009356

For my father, Dr. Jack M. Stein,
who showed me very early in life that work is both
meaningful and fun. He mirrored to me that there
is no greater gift to give to the world than freely
giving the gift you have.

# CONTENTS

# ACKNOWLEDGMENTS

Thank you Melissa, Rusty, Jill, and Saundra for always being there. I appreciate all of the efforts that the publishers, editors, and marketing staff at McGraw-Hill have made to help my book be successful. I especially appreciate the discerning contributions of my editor, Donya Dickerson.

# INTRODUCTION

Have you been thinking about making a career change? Would you rather be doing something you love instead of something you just "fell into"? Perhaps your company downsized and you're out of work. Regardless of why you want to change careers, now may be the perfect time to start thinking about something new.

The idea of making a career transition may sound appetizing, but the reality could be a bit uncertain—even scary. Perhaps you've thought that changing careers sounded great but found yourself wary of taking action because

- It just doesn't seem practical to you.
- It would probably cost too much anyway.
- You don't want to have to wait years to amass new education and experience.
- You're afraid of failure or even success!

> *Or, if you feel fearful about making a move for any other reason, this book was written for you!*

It doesn't have to take a year or more to begin working in a career you love. In fact, I'll show you how to do it in about 90 days and for less of an investment than you've ever imagined. *Fearless Career Change* guides you easily, rapidly, and economically through a process of identifying and actually getting a real dream job in the real world. Through this book,

- You'll see the strategies with which hundreds of my own career counseling clients found a career in a field they loved in a matter of a few months or less.

- You'll discover the secrets that have worked for people of all ages—entry level to executive, artsy to technical. They've even worked for people who didn't think they had the skills to enter a new occupation.

- You'll find that some of the people I'll introduce to you have made radical and rapid career transitions for less than it costs for a tank of gas.

Yes, it's possible to begin designing your own new career now. In my 13 years plus as a career coach, I've seen this happen time after time. Take Maria, who went from being a gardener to an environmental planner (while tripling her salary) and did it in *less than three weeks and for a sum of about $450.*

Then there's Scott, an insurance salesperson who broke into the film industry in just *one* day with just one perfectly phrased phone call and with his bank account virtually untouched.

You'll learn the strategies that Alice used to double her salary in less than a month (for about $300 and two days of intensive training) by going from sitting behind a desk to delivering babies for a living.

And how Nancy went from being a public health official to a book editor for just $50 in about three months. You'll find plenty of examples of people who have made transitions just like the one you may make, and you'll discover, blow by blow, exactly how they did it and exactly how you can do it too.

## *My Career Change Success Story*

Despite the perceived difficulties in changing careers, billions of us do. The U.S. Bureau of Labor (www.bls.gov) statistics estimates that the average American adult will change *jobs* from five to seven times and change *careers* from three to five times in his or her life.

I myself have already had numerous jobs, and I've changed careers three times. When I say "jobs," I'm referring to a set of duties I perform in exchange for a paycheck. When I use the word "career," I am referring to an ongoing learning experience in a field that I deliberately advance in and enjoy, while making a living.

One day, when I was between careers and not sure of what move to make next, I picked up a book that would change my life. It was called *Wishcraft*, and it was written by a now very prominent author and television personality named Barbara Sher.* (Ms. Sher has some fascinating ideas about careers and career changes on her Web site at www.barbarasher.com.) When I read Sher's *Wishcraft*, it seemed completely different from other books I had seen about career change.

I thought about my next career change for quite some time, and one day, I decided I wanted to become a career counselor. It seemed odd, at first, that something I always enjoyed doing at parties (asking people about their careers) could be something I could be paid for.

I enrolled in a three-day course about teaching job search methods, and I became a Certified Job Search Trainer for about $250. I interviewed 10 different career counselors, and *all* of them told me that I would never make it as a career counselor without a master's degree and that there was too much competition in my area.

Fortunately, I scheduled a visit to see a very wise career counselor. When I told her about how much I wanted to be a career counselor and when I related the negative information that others had given me, she had only one thing to say to me, *"If that's where your heart is, then do it."* So I did.

Despite all the negative reports, I set out to make it possible for me to make this career change. I enrolled in a master's level class in counseling (for about $350) at a local university that allowed open enrollment. If I did not already have a graduate degree, at least I could *create the perception* that I was in the midst of getting one. And it worked.

I did a four-month internship at a local government agency before I started out as a professional. Despite all of the people who said I had to have a master's degree, I have, to date, coached over 10,000 clients, worked as a career consultant for the top two career management firms in the world, and become known for my writings on career topics around the world.

## The Fearless Career Change Process

In the next chapters we're going to pinpoint the exact strategies that many others have used to make swift but meaningful

* Barbara Sher (with Annie Gottlieb), *Wishcraft, How to Get What You Really Want*, 2d ed., Ballantine Books/Random House, New York, 2003.

career changes. The first three chapters of the book are crafted to help you decide "from the inside out" what career most closely matches your natural talents and gifts. We'll also talk about getting over the fear of taking a risk and how you can condition yourself for success.

Making a career change is going to involve both thought and action from you. Too often, fear can cause a kind of paralysis that prohibits positive action and even inhibits constructive thought. That kind of paralysis can lead to procrastination, bury our dreams, or even bring us to a screeching halt.

Many of the exercises in the book are designed to beat your fear by

- Identifying just what is stopping you.
- Reminding you of constructive ways you've dealt with fear before.
- Applying the positive attributes *you already have* to breaking through the obstacle of fear.
- Showing you the methods by which other real people have beat their fear and moved on to great careers.
- Getting you on the right path of decisive action toward the career goals you set for yourself.

The middle of the book will carefully illustrate how, in little time and with little money you can actually make the transition from where you are now to where you'd like to be. You'll learn eight strategies that will propel you to your new position with ease.

Finally, I'll let you in on the *fastest* techniques, based on many years of research, to actually break into your new field and get a job offer or start your own business. We'll take it step by step, together.

You'll be able to pick the particular styles and techniques that suit your personality and preferences. Used alone, or in combination, these techniques will propel you to passionate and powerful career choices, and help you design a map that shows you how to get there.

CHAPTER ONE

# Overcoming Your Fears

## Signs of Change

While some people find a career change to be exhilarating, others may experience the uncertainty of the transition as terrifying. But for people in both categories, the first question often is, How do you know it's time to change? If you're still employed, you may have noticed the stirrings of mild discontent with your work have finally become so pronounced that they cannot be ignored. Going to a different job in the same field won't fix the problem. You might come to realize that a more profound change is needed.

The end of a career may start with feelings of uneasiness or frustration or even depression. These feelings may fester into burnout and exhaustion, or they may take the form of self-sabotaging behavior like being late to work or not meeting deadlines. Or, for some people, the need to change careers comes more rapidly through a sudden occurrence like a layoff. These people have to face an event that is out of their control and that is significantly disruptive. Perhaps their whole field or profession is temporarily dormant or struggling, and they have to find an entirely new way of making a living.

The signals that a career may be coming to an end may appear in unexpected ways, as in a dream. The need to cease what you're doing or how you're doing it may manifest as physical symptoms, such as tendonitis, neck pain, or back pain, or as psychophysical issues like overindulgence with food or alcohol, problems with sleeping, gastrointestinal problems, or sexual difficulties.

For some people, there is no precipitating event that forces them to change careers. Instead, there is perhaps just a faint whisper in the soul that "there *must* be something better." At some point, often quite spontaneously, these same people summon the courage to embark on doing something they've always wanted to do.

> **Your career change need not be turbulent or dramatic. It may just be part of a natural cycle, and it may happen more than once.**

If you're like many people, you've thought of what it might be like to have that "something better," but you may be putting it off until the kids go to school, your savings account is fuller, you have an advanced degree, the kids are out of college, you lose 10 pounds, you get married (or divorced), your parents, spouse, or kids approve, the economy picks up, or scores of other reasons.

The problem, though, with waiting until later is that sometimes later never comes. You keep putting it off and putting it off until, one day, you may wake up when you're 5 or 15 years older and agonize over what you *could* have done or what you *should* have done.

> **By reading this book, you're taking the first steps toward a future designed by wants, not by shoulds.**

## Common Fears about Career Change

In a word, change itself (even change for the better) can be scary and stressful. Two opposing needs—one for the security of the job you've known, and one for the freedom to choose a job that might be better—seem at odds with each other. It's frustrating to be pulled in two directions and easy to become overwhelmed and even afraid of the prospect of change.

Take a look at some common and very understandable fears I've heard my clients express when faced with the prospect of exploring a new and different occupation. If you, too, have one or more of the following fears, we're going to take a serious look at them in this chapter and utilize some techniques that can help you get around and through them.

- "Every time I mention my dream career to people, they say it's too competitive and I'm safer where I am."

- "I think I'm too young to change careers. What if I look like I'm 'job hopping'?"

- "I don't have the money to go back to school to get an advanced degree."

- "I really want a new career, but I'm afraid my savings account or severance pay will wear out before I find a new position."

- "If I have to show up at my present job for one more day, I'm going to explode with boredom (or stress). The trouble is, I have no idea about what I want to do next!"

- "I'd like to be a _____, but I don't think I'd meet the requirements."

- "I've dreamed so long about being a _____, but I'm afraid I'll fail."

- "I absolutely *hate* my job, but if I just stay a little bit longer, I'll get a bonus. I'll just think about a career change *next* year."

- "I'm completely stuck. I have several careers in mind, but I don't want to pick the wrong one. Maybe I'll just wait for a sudden inspiration."

- "I'm too old. *Nobody* starts a new business at age 74."

- "I've always wanted to be a _____, but a (parent, teacher, friend, guidance counselor) told me I would never make it."

- "If I become a big success at my new job, my friends will get jealous and reject me."

- "If I had a new career where I felt *really* happy, I don't think I could handle it. I'd have nothing to worry about anymore."

Every single person I have met who is struggling with making a career change is either limited by fear of some sort or lack of information. This chapter will help you use victories in your past to neutralize your fears and sculpt the triumphs of tomorrow. Then Chapter 3 will aid you in finding the right information to make an informed choice about your next venture.

You probably have specific fears that aren't on the list above. In either case, it helps to write them down so you know what you are up against.

My three most pressing concerns about making a career change:

1. _____
_____
_____

2. _____
_____
_____

3. _____
_____
_____

Another fear, not on the list:

4. _____
_____
_____

Another fear, not on the list:

5. _____
_____
_____

## Fear of Failure

Most of us have the wrong idea when it comes to failure. Do you know how many times a baby falls before she takes that first step that launches her out onto her own? Do we call her first attempts "failures" just because she ends up on the floor? Of course not, and neither does she. She gets up and tries again! I've heard the story of Thomas Edison, the genius who invented the lightbulb, many times. According to the story, Edison's friend approached him and said, "Why in the world do you stay in your laboratory, trying time and time again to make that thing work when you've failed a thousand times already?" Edison purportedly answered, "No, you're wrong—it's been 10,000 times, and I've succeeded every single time in finding yet another way not to make a lightbulb!" Think how many millions of households and factories might have had to manage with candlelight for another hundred years had there not been a man as brave as Edison. He truly "reframed" the meaning of the word *failure* into something more like a "lesson"—and a successful one at that. The fear of failure can be so constricting that you lose the confidence and the ability to take risks—and you must have both qualities if you're going to make a successful career change. My bet is that, even if you don't have confidence now or you are hesitant to take a risk, there was a time in your life when you were unafraid. We're going to uncover some of those times in the next exercise.

For the first exercise, take a look at one of the fears you listed above, and ask yourself these questions in relation to that fear.

1. What is the worst thing that can happen if I change careers?

    _____

    _____

    _____

2. What's the best thing that can happen?

    _____

    _____

    _____

3. How likely is it that the worst thing will happen?

    _____

    _____

    _____

4. How would I solve the problem if the worst thing did happen?

   _____

   _____

   _____

5. What steps could I take now to prevent the worst thing from happening?

   _____

   _____

   _____

6. How will I feel about myself if the best thing happens?

   _____

   _____

   _____

7. What steps can I take to ensure that the best thing happens?

   _____

   _____

   _____

8. If I look back on my life one year from now, I will be glad that I (describe an action here).

   _____

   _____

   _____

9. If I look back on my life 15 years from now, I'll see that making the choice now to _____

   _____ was a good one.

Career changes are not just about skill, timing, and the latest strategies. They're about mental focus, passionate motivation, and sometimes trust in things or people that we didn't even know we had before. Career changes demand a great deal of heroism, as almost every career change I've witnessed involved not only some sort of temporary sacrifice or uncertainty followed by some sort of triumph, however small or great, but also some kind of risk. If you have survived this long in this complex and demanding world, you are bound to have taken at least one risk.

# *Taking Risks*

Let's do an exercise to find out how you did it and how you can do it again.

What are three risks I've taken in my life that have had a positive outcome for me? Describe exactly what happened before and after the positive risk and *your role* in making it turn out favorably.

1. _____

   _____

2. _____

   _____

3. _____

   _____

Ask yourself, "What do these three risks have in common? What mental attitudes and emotional attributes do they have in common? What do they say about me?" Write your answer here:

_____

_____

_____

Finally, write a paragraph or more about why you would like to make a career transition right now. Write both the negatives of your last or present job and the positives you hope for in your next job.

_____

_____

_____

You probably noticed some patterns in the successful risks you took, and you may have discovered some personal attributes that you hadn't really thought of before.

> *Career changes are not only about doing the right things to bring about a change. They are also about being the person it takes to weather the fears, the victories, and the ups and downs of profound change.*

Here is a list of some of the personal qualities that successful career changers possess. Make a check next to the particular attributes you've noticed in these exercises or the ones that you believe you possess.

- ❏ Adaptability
- ❏ Confidence
- ❏ Courage
- ❏ Creativity
- ❏ Determination
- ❏ Drive
- ❏ Faith
- ❏ Flexibility
- ❏ Honesty
- ❏ Logic
- ❏ Motivation

- ❏ Open-mindedness
- ❏ Passion
- ❏ Perseverance (persistence in the face of "failure")
- ❏ Persistence
- ❏ Problem-solving skills
- ❏ Rationality
- ❏ Resourcefulness
- ❏ Sense of humor
- ❏ Vision
- ❏ Willingness

You don't have to have all of these attributes to achieve favorable results. In fact, if you have just one, you will have enough. When we get to Chapter 8, I would like you to look back on this list and see the richness you have to draw from. Looking at this list and consciously bringing one of your personal attributes to the forefront will help you make tough choices and weather temporary setbacks.

## Building a Transition Income

Understandably, many people's fears about changing careers center on having enough money to make it through a period of unemployment and perhaps training between jobs. Most people have considerably less anxiety when they are going through this process with the cushion of a little money in the bank. Typically three months' salary would be the bare minimum to have before changing careers, although many people who haven't had more than a penny saved have had smooth transitions to a new career.

To determine how much you'll need to feel comfortable, let's build what I call a *transition income*. Take a moment to think about the *necessities* in your life, and distinguish them from your *preferences*. *Necessities* are things you absolutely must have for shelter, nutrition, health, sanity, and other basic needs.

Some examples of necessities for many of us are:

- Rent
- Mortgage
- Food
- Furniture
- Automobile insurance
- Vehicle maintenance and repair
- Pet care
- Medical and dental care
- Phone
- Transportation
- Taxes
- Cell phone
- Some degree of social and entertainment activities
- Home maintenance and repair
- Child care
- Elder care
- Gas and electric service
- An "emergency fund"
- Debt consolidation
- Money for gifts and holidays
- Retirement savings or investments
- Tithing to your church or temple
- And whatever else you need to feel comfortable

*Preferences* are things that enhance your lifestyle—goodies like cable or satellite TV, a state-of-the-art home entertainment system, one or more luxury cars, extensive travel, preventive health care, a housekeeper, a gardener or landscaper, a vast CD or DVD collection, a handsome wardrobe, a gym membership, charitable contributions, vacations, exercise equipment, massage, concerts, ballet, high-speed Internet connections, membership to a country club, wireless handheld devices, a fully stocked home workshop, video equipment, expensive cameras, new kitchenware, linens, or home décor, a second car for yourself or your family, first-class travel, extensive investments and retirement income, a pool—you get the picture.

Now that the difference is clear, take a minute to think about the following: What do you want, when do you want them, and what will be the cost of enjoying those things?

Please use this section to list your absolute necessities for at least a three-month period. (You may want to refer to the lists above so you don't leave anything out.) Then, do your best to estimate the monthly (and quarterly) costs of each of the items you chose. For example:

| | |
|---|---|
| Mortgage | $1,000 |
| Monthly housekeeper | 90 |
| Car payment | 250 |

Fixed costs (costs that remain the same from month to month like a mortgage, rent, or car payment):

1. _____
2. _____
3. _____
4. _____
5. _____
6. _____
7. _____
8. _____
9. _____

Variable expenses (the phone, electric, and gas bills):

10. _____
11. _____

12. _____
13. _____
14. _____
15. _____
16. _____
17. _____
18. _____
19. _____
20. _____

When you're finished, total the amount.

Total    $ _____ per month

_____ per quarter (1 month × 3)

What amount do you think you could live on, *at minimum*, for 3 months? $ _____

| | |
|---|---|
| 6 months? | $ _____ |
| 9 months? | $ _____ |
| A year? | $ _____ |

It may take 90 days to a year to make your career transition, especially if you need to get some extra training, wait for your new small business to turn a profit, or establish your value in a new job so that you get a raise. If you decide on a career that takes two or more years of education, you will of course have to save or earn the money that will pay for your living expenses and education in the interim.

Take a look at your expense list again and consider it as carefully as you wish. Think about things you may be able to put aside for a while, thereby saving some extra cash for yourself as you make your way through the process of changing occupations. For example, you could use public transportation instead of putting wear and tear on the car.

You'd be surprised by how you can cut corners a bit and barely even notice it, especially if you know it's only for a limited time. You probably won't have or want to give up *all* your luxuries at once.

---

> **Would giving up three or four of those costly items be worth the joy you're going to feel when you're doing a job you love, coming home energized, feeling great about yourself, and working your way (back) to the top of a new field where you really want to be?**

---

*Your happiness is urgent.* Fear may be at the back door, but you don't have to let it in. You've conquered risks before. You have what it takes to succeed. What waits for you on the other side of apprehension and procrastination is the indescribable joy of being in the right place, doing the right job at the right time. And the time is now!

# CHAPTER TWO

# Creating Your Career Fingerprint

By far the most satisfying careers spring not just from what we want or what we are interested in but from what we were truly meant to do. How do you know what you were meant to do? Finding the answer involves becoming aware of your *authentic calling*, which many people see as divinely or naturally inscribed on your genetic code and imprinted on your soul. This chapter is called "Creating Your Career Fingerprint" because each one of us possesses a unique authentic calling, a metaphorical fingerprint, if you will, of the right career for us, unlike that of anyone else's in the world. We each have a special stamp to make in the world, however bold or faint to the eye.

> *Each of us has an unrepeatable calling or combination of natural and unique talents in this lifetime, and it's up to us to discover them and celebrate them. Expressing your natural and unique talents outwardly, in one way or another, can lead to a kind of happiness and peace that few other experiences can rival.*

Finding your authentic calling (or special talent) may sound a little bit mysterious. From my experience, though, I can safely say that given the right circumstances, your own calling will come tumbling off your tongue and you'll wonder how it was you didn't notice it in the first place. When you are operating from your calling, it will, indeed, seem like you are not working at all but rather simply and almost magically, flowing. In my 13 years of being a career coach, I have very rarely had a client who, given the right prompting (as you'll have in this book), could not state his or her special talent within 10 or 20 minutes after talking with me. People who have done the exercises presented in this book have reported to me that, even though they were unsure of their career direction, it became clear to them as a result of gaining enormous self-knowledge from completing these exercises.

---

**If the word calling *seems unnatural to you for any reason, try substituting the words* natural ability *or* talent.**

---

You probably know your calling *now*—it may just take a little coaxing and my assurance to you that it's there and that you should get it down on paper. That's what the process that I call *career fingerprinting* is about: finding that single thing—a talent, a power, a special genius—that (like a fingerprint) is unique to you and only you. That's what we'll be doing in the following exercises.

## What Is My Authentic Calling?

In this first exercise in the career fingerprinting process, complete each one of the following phrases using the first thing that pops into your mind. You may rest at ease even if your answers seem to make no sense at all because we're going to spend time together for the rest of this book making sure that your answers translate into a real-world career that you can fully enjoy. Right now, we're just at the beginning. There's no right or wrong answer. It doesn't matter if your answers are all the same, all different, or some sort of mixture. Try not to analyze it at all. We'll have plenty of time for analysis later. For now, let yourself have some fun.

**You are about to encounter the wild, unencumbered self that you are—the self you would be if you had absolutely no barriers, responsibilities, past disappointments, issues with money, or future worries—and complete these sentences as if you had no limitations whatsoever and without censoring.**

When I was a child, I was naturally talented at

_____

_____

_____

Someone once told me I was particularly talented at

_____

_____

_____

Other people have told me that I was unusually adept at

_____

_____

_____

If I asked the wisest man or woman in the world "What is my special talent?" he or she would say, "Your special talent is

_____

_____

_____

and you can use it to

_____

_____

_____

If I came to know the kindest man or woman in the universe, he or she would tell me that my authentic calling is

_____

_____

_____

and I can use it to

_____

_____

_____

Two years from now it will be clear that my authentic calling has always been

_____

_____

_____

Five years from now it will dawn on me that my calling has always been

_____

_____

_____

Ten years from now I'll realize that my calling is

_____

_____

_____

Twenty years from now I'll look back and I will see that my calling was or is

_____

_____

_____

Thirty years from now I'll reflect upon my life and know that my calling was

_____

_____

_____

When I die, the people who knew me will say I was uniquely talented at

_____

_____

_____

and I used my talent(s) to

_____

_____

_____

I believe my authentic calling is

_____

_____

_____

I have no idea at all what my calling is, but I'd like to pretend that it is

_____

_____

_____

A little "voice" in my head says my authentic calling is

_____

_____

_____

If my vision of my calling were to become crystal clear, it would look like

_____

_____

_____

I cannot find the words to express my natural and unique talent, but if I pretend now that I can hear the words, they would be saying

_____

_____

_____

People in the past have "made fun" of my natural and unique talent, but I now have the courage and strength to say that it is

_____

_____

_____

and I'm going to use it to

_____

_____

_____

In my most private moments, I really know that my authentic calling is

_____

_____

_____

## Fifteen Categories of Unique and Special Talents

Did you have an easy or a difficult time doing the preceding exercise? If it seemed difficult to pinpoint exactly what your special talent is, that's okay. We'll soon explore several categories of unique abilities that you may recognize in yourself. If you found that the answers to the prompts were very easy for you, you may skip to the next chapter if you wish.

To start pinpointing your authentic calling, go through the following categories of talents as if you had no limitations, and see if any of them might include something that appeals to you. You may relate to many, one, or none of these gifts. It really doesn't matter. In the long run, *all you need is one.* By the end of this section you will have identified the one(s) most important to you.

---

**If for some reason the specific talent that you believe you have is not on this list, then by all means write down your own version of your natural ability in your own words.**

---

❑ Are you good at making people feel genuinely important?

*Do you have a natural talent for listening so intently that you are able to block out all external stimuli just to focus on whomever you're talking to? Can you give sincere compliments and uplifting comments to people that help them feel important and understood? Do you make it a habit to see and bring out the best in people? Do people tend to naturally trust you?*

A few careers associated with this talent could be

- Astrologer
- Customer service representative
- Drug and alcohol counselor
- Human resources director
- Life coach
- Medical doctor
- Psychotherapist
- Real estate agent
- Registered nurse

❑ Are you good at assisting people in healing or personal growth?

*Do you seem to naturally feel empathy and compassion for people? Do you gravitate toward those whom you can help? Do you feel delight when people feel better or improve their performance as a result of interacting with you? Do you thrive on inspiring and motivating others?*

A few careers associated with this talent could be

- Acupuncturist
- Certified neurolinguistic programmer
- Chiropractor
- Family nurse practitioner
- Health columnist
- Herbalist
- Member of the clergy
- Midwife
- Motivational speaker
- Personal athletic trainer
- Psychic or intuitive
- Psychologist, therapist, or counselor

❑ Are you good at persuading people?

*Do you have a way with bringing people around to your point of view? Do you have an innate sense of what people want or what they would find attractive? Do people tend to trust you and believe what you say? Have you ever completely changed a person's mind from one viewpoint to an opposite one? Do you enjoy when people seek you out for advice?*

A few careers associated with this talent could be

- Actor
- Advertising salesperson
- Consultant, counselor, or personal coach
- Graphic artist
- Magazine, book, or newspaper writer, editor, or publisher
- Marketing and communications specialist
- Personal financial planner
- Politician or political activist
- Professor or teacher
- Public speaker
- Salesperson
- Supervisor

❑ Are you good at designing things?

*Do you thrive on designing simple or complex things, processes, or projects? Is it second nature for you to be organized in anything you undertake? Do you have an eye for the big picture but also a sense for the minutest details? Do you love to orchestrate different elements to create a new and functional, logical, or aesthetic whole?*

A few careers associated with this talent could be

- Biochemist
- Computer-aided drafter
- Events planner
- Fashion designer
- Food stylist (film and photography)
- Interior decorator
- Landscape architect
- Mechanical engineer
- Programmer analyst
- Software programmer
- Window dresser for a store

❑ Are you good at building things?

*Do you love to work with your hands and wood, stone, metal, plants, or other materials? Do the acts of sculpting, smoothing, cutting, digging, lifting, moving, or painting appeal to you? Do you enjoy jobs and recreational pursuits in which all or part of your body can get involved? Do you like to figure out how things fit together and create, enhance, reinforce, restore, or repair them?*

A few careers associated with this talent could be

- Aircraft engineer
- Auto mechanic
- Computer or office machine repair
- Construction supervisor
- Electronics manufacturer
- Fine arts sculptor
- Fine cabinetry maker
- Gardener or landscaper
- Surgeon
- Watch repairer

❑ Do you enjoy operating things?

*Do you think that you may learn how to operate machinery faster or more easily than most people do? Do you enjoy the rhythm of operating a small or large machine correctly and efficiently? Do you think you have more patience than most people when you operate machines? Do machines, toys, and gadgets fascinate you?*

A few careers associated with this talent could be

- Assembly line worker
- Commercial airline pilot
- Digital video editor
- Heavy-machinery operator
- Lighting technician

- Office manager
- Photographer
- Respiratory therapist
- Sound technician

- Truck driver
- Ultrasound technician
- Word processor

❑ Are you especially adept at fixing things?

*Can you quickly analyze a situation, product, or project and come up with a solution to repair, restore, or improve it? Are you able to take many factors into account and arrive at a workable solution? Are you able to observe things, people, and processes objectively? Do you feel confident about your ability to solve problems, and do you derive satisfaction from troubleshooting difficult or not-so-obvious challenges?*

A few careers associated with this talent could be

- Appliance repairer
- Automotive repairer
- Business consultant
- Car detailer
- Certified heat and air-conditioning technician
- Financial advisor

- Organizational consultant
- Plumber
- Postsales hardware engineer
- Professional mediator
- Small business machine repair

❑ Do you love to test and stretch your intellect as far as you can possibly go?

*If your appetite for knowledge about a particular scientific or artistic field is nearly insatiable, you may want to apply your intellect to learning as much as you can about a given subject. Would you like to be considered an expert in your field? Would you like to write, research, or illuminate a certain topic or topics? Have you ever noticed that you never tire of reading everything you can find about a certain subject? Do you enjoy being in an academic environment and/or discussing intellectual pursuits with like-minded people? Do you attend lectures just for fun? Do you feel most comfortable in a laboratory, editing room, library, or classroom?*

A few careers associated with this talent could be

- Biophysicist
- Environmental planner
- Fiction or nonfiction writer
- Filmmaker
- Historian

- Marine biologist
- Mathematician
- Music composer
- Political analyst
- Research scientist
- Sociologist

❑ Are you gifted with unusual physical strength, agility, grace, coordination, or fine motor skills?

*Do you enjoy using talents that highlight your physical strength, agility, or coordination? Are you careful to take very good care of your body? Is it important to you to excel physically and mentally at what you do? Do you sometimes notice that you're competitive? Are you more dedicated and disciplined than most people about your physical health and/or appearance?*

A few careers associated with this talent could be

- Athlete
- Athletic coach
- Dancer
- Entertainer
- Massage therapist

- Personal trainer
- Pilates instructor
- Stunt man or woman
- Yoga instructor

❑ Do you have a burning desire to share your compassion, love, and empathy with the world?

*Is it extremely important to you to make a contribution in the world or a difference in the lives of individuals? Would you like to be a pivotal person in someone's growth, development, or even happiness? Do you feel driven to leave the legacy of being a loving and caring person? Do you ever have the sense that you are somehow divinely mandated to give something back to humanity, even if it means that you may not make hoards of money? Do you genuinely love being around people and rarely tire of them?*

A few careers associated with this talent could be

- Artist
- Author or journalist
- Child-care worker
- Director of a nonprofit
- Entertainer
- Homeless advocate
- Life or career coach
- Lobbyist
- Minister
- Motivational speaker
- Physician's assistant
- Political advocate or activist
- Psychotherapist
- Senior citizen companion
- Teacher
- Volunteer

❑ Are you so incredibly adept with detail that you amaze your family and friends?

*Do you get great satisfaction from striving for absolute perfection? Do you feel a sense of pride when you have created order out of chaos and/or organization from disarray? Is it easy and natural for you to work slowly and methodically so that you end with a perfect result? Do you have more patience than most people with detail? Can other people trust you to put things in tidy, logical order? Do you thrive on efficiency?*

A few careers associated with this talent could be

- Accountant
- Archaeologist
- Assembler
- Bookkeeper
- Building inspector
- Clean-room specialist
- Database analyst
- Financial analyst
- Forensic expert
- House cleaner
- Insurance agent
- Laboratory technician
- Logistics manager
- Operations director
- Property appraiser
- Research scientist
- Surgeon
- Watch repairer

❑ Are you mathematically gifted?

*Do numbers, diagrams, and numerical concepts come easily—are they fun? Do you love to work on easy or increasingly difficult numerical or geometric puzzles? Do mathematics or numbers represent something beautiful to you? Do you think you are more adept with numbers than the average person is? Can you immediately spot errors in mathematical calculations and correct them?*

A few careers associated with this talent could be

- Astrophysicist
- Biophysicist
- Bookkeeper
- Business manager
- Certified public accountant
- Chemist
- Chief financial officer
- Controller
- Engineer
- Executive
- Mathematics instructor
- Mortgage broker
- Software programmer
- Stockbroker
- Tax preparer

❑ Are you gifted at leading, managing, or directing large-scale projects?

*Do you love to pull together all of the resources necessary to produce a desired result? Do people seem to look to you when the chips are down? Do you feel that you have a special way of looking at things and doing things that makes you a good leader? Can you get other people to follow your vision or act on your ideas? Do you ever dream of starting a company of your own? Do you think you know how to bring out the best in people?*

A few careers associated with this talent could be

- Art director
- Commercial building contractor
- Corporate or small-business executive
- Department supervisor, manager, or director
- Events planner
- Producer or director (theater, film, television, music)
- Production manager
- Program or project manager
- Trade show coordinator
- Travel agent
- Wedding planner

❑ Do you have a scientific or academic bent?

*Do you love to dig into research and compare or create theories? Do you love to apply the scientific method to do experiments and conduct research? Are you interested in subjects that others might consider esoteric? Do you have hypotheses you'd like to test and then publish the results? Are you drawn to pure science? Do you find beauty in science? Do you often find yourself wishing that you could just spend time alone reading, for days at a time?*

A few careers associated with this talent could be

- Anthropologist
- Archaeologist
- Biographer
- Chemist
- Ethnographer
- Ethnomusicologist
- Experimental psychologist
- Geologist
- Historian
- Paleontologist
- Physicist
- Psychopharmacologist

❑ Are you an expert at taking physical, intellectual, emotional, and/or financial risks?

*Does playing for high stakes and not knowing your outcome give you a rush? Do you thrive on pressure and do your best under stress? Do you like to be the underdog who comes out ahead at the last moment? Do you enjoy an adrenaline rush and sometimes wonder why other people are so slow? Do you live for the next challenge? Are you attracted to dangerous situations, and do you feel confident that you can do just about anything you put your mind to?*

A few careers associated with this talent could be

- Adventure guide
- Boat, horse, car, windsurfing, or bicycle racer
- Entrepreneur or small-business owner
- Firefighter
- Inventor
- Military officer
- Mountaineering instructor
- Police officer or detective
- Private investigator
- Small-airplane operator
- Stand-up comedian
- Stocks and bonds investor
- Whitewater rafting guide

❑ Are you artistically gifted?

*Do you crave the opportunity to create beauty and symbolism in the world? Can a symphony, painting, or sculpture move you to tears? Have others told you that you have a gift for being artistic? Can you remember wanting to be an artist, actor, or musician since you were very young? Have people ever said that they appreciated or were moved by something you made or did? Have you always known you were an artist but kept it hidden because it seemed impractical or someone criticized you? Do you think that art is one of the most important things in the world?*

A few careers associated with this talent could be

- Actor
- Clothing, manufacturing, or furniture designer
- Crafts designer
- Dancer
- Film, theater, or television director
- Fine artist
- Florist
- Graphic or Web designer
- Interior decorator
- Musician
- Playwright
- Sculptor
- Singer

You may find that one or more special talents in these sections really resonate with you. For example, you may love to make people feel genuinely important *and* you may also be particularly talented at managing or leading large-scale projects. Write down one, two, or three of the above talents (or choose ones you believe you have that may not appear in the above list), beginning with the one you believe is the strongest.

At this time I think or feel that my authentic calling is

1. _____ and I know this because

_____

_____

_____

2. _____ and I know this because

_____

3. _____ and I know this because

_____

Perhaps you found even three or more callings that apply to you. That's fine. You may be a multiply gifted person. We'll discover some guideposts in the next section that will point the way to your particular path.

## Applying Your Gifts in the Real World

If you have an authentic calling for being persuasive, for example, it is doubtful that someone will pay you simply for that raw talent. Your calling must somehow be put in context by becoming part of the world in which people are paid to perform meaningful jobs. Being persuasive, for example, might be translated into the world of work as a specific job title that is generally recognized and that people receive monetary compensation for. Some jobs that match well with the calling of being persuasive are teacher, minister, attorney, salesperson, and actor.

---

*In the next exercise you'll be scanning through a list of job titles and asking yourself the question, "How well would this job title allow me to express my authentic calling?"*

---

With this exercise, it's important to really let your imagination and intuition flow freely. It may even mean that you suspend, for a while, your normal, rational, critical mind in order to give other, deeper, and perhaps wiser, parts of your being a chance to bring forth messages you may not have considered before. Some people call this frame of mind "thinking out of the box," and others, "emotional intelligence." Let your mind and feelings be as flexible as possible. Too often our critical minds are the culprits that landed us in jobs we found to be unfulfilling. Now is your chance to let what I call your "deeper mind" choose for you!

> ***If you haven't already seen a clear picture of your authentic calling, the following exercise will give important clues to assist you in clarifying your vision.***

This exercise assesses how your gifts fit into the real world of jobs. You may believe that your career needs to be *bold, heroic,* or a *status symbol* to the rest of the world. This is not the case, because when you come upon the right career for you at this time in your life, you will *feel* fantastic no matter how the world evaluates your occupation. When you are expressing something from deep inside of you through the work you choose to do, you are making a maximum contribution both to yourself and to the world. You will be living the life you are meant to live in your own quiet way. You'll be proud of yourself. You will *know* you are magnificent! We have no time to waste, so let's begin.

1. Consider the list of occupations that is provided in the next few pages of this chapter. Look at every occupation from A to Z. There are lots of entries in the list, so you might want to try this exercise in two or three sittings.

2. Circle any entry (for example, dog shampooer, event planner, filmmaker, lawyer, pediatrician, software programmer, technician, vice president, Web designer) that you feel would allow you to express your gifts. The assumption here is that you already have all the right amount of money, education, time, familial support, location, and physical and mental ability to actually try that role for a short time. In other words, just for the sake of this exercise, you have no limitations.

3. Next, go through the occupations list again and check only those listings you would be willing to try for a whole year, again with the assumption that you are completely equipped to do them. Place a check by those job titles, whether they are circled or not.

4. Finally, pick 10 of these job titles that are both circled and checked.

At the end of this list, you'll have space to write down your 10 selections. Go for it!

# Occupations List

## A

- ❑ Abortion counselor
- ❑ Accountant
- ❑ Acupuncturist
- ❑ Addiction counselor
- ❑ Adjuster, insurance
- ❑ Administrator, health
- ❑ Administrator, office
- ❑ Administrator, school
- ❑ Administrator, unspecified
- ❑ Adoption counselor
- ❑ Adult assisted living coordinator
- ❑ Adult education teacher
- ❑ Aerial photographer
- ❑ Aeronautical researcher
- ❑ Agricultural worker
- ❑ Airbrush artist
- ❑ Alarm installer
- ❑ Alzheimer's counselor
- ❑ Ambulance driver
- ❑ Anesthesiologist
- ❑ Animal trainer
- ❑ Animator, film and video
- ❑ Antique store owner
- ❑ Apartment manager
- ❑ Appliance repairer
- ❑ Appraiser, real estate
- ❑ Aquatic researcher
- ❑ Architect
- ❑ Armed forces member, enlisted
- ❑ Army member, enlisted
- ❑ Art appraiser
- ❑ Art critic
- ❑ Art museum curator
- ❑ Asbestos consultant
- ❑ Assembler
- ❑ Assistant editor
- ❑ Astrologer
- ❑ Astronomer
- ❑ Astrophysicist
- ❑ Athlete
- ❑ Athletic trainer, certified
- ❑ Attorney
- ❑ Audio engineer
- ❑ Audiologist
- ❑ Author
- ❑ Automobile design
- ❑ Automobile repairer
- ❑ Automobile salesperson
- ❑ Automotive technician, smog
- ❑ Aviator

## B

- ❑ Babysitter
- ❑ Backpacking guide
- ❑ Baker
- ❑ Bakery owner
- ❑ Ballroom dancing teacher

❑ Bankruptcy consultant
❑ Baseball player
❑ Beauty salon owner
❑ Bed-and-breakfast manager
❑ Behavioral scientist
❑ Benefits, human resources
❑ Bereavement counselor
❑ Bibliographer
❑ Biochemist
❑ Biofeedback therapist
❑ Biographer
❑ Biologist
❑ Biomechanical engineer
❑ Biopharmaceutical scientist
❑ Biophysicist
❑ Birth coach
❑ Birth control counselor
❑ Blind persons support
❑ Blinds, cleaning service owner
❑ Bodybuilder, professional
❑ Bodybuilder, instructor
❑ Bodyguard
❑ Bookkeeper
❑ Broker, automobile
❑ Broker, real estate
❑ Broker, stocks and bonds
❑ Builder, construction
❑ Building code consultant
❑ Building inspector
❑ Bus driver, school or public
❑ Business consultant

❑ Business owner, unspecified
❑ Butcher
❑ Buyer

# C

❑ Cabinetmaker
❑ Camera operator, film and video
❑ Campground manager
❑ Candy store owner
❑ Career counselor
❑ Carpenter
❑ Carpet seller, retail or wholesale
❑ Cashier
❑ Casino manager
❑ Casting director, film and TV
❑ Caterer
❑ Certified financial planner
❑ Certified personal trainer
❑ Certified public account
❑ Chairman of the board
❑ Chauffeur
❑ Chef
❑ Chemist
❑ Chief executive officer
❑ Chief financial officer
❑ Chief information officer
❑ Chief operating officer
❑ Chief technical officer
❑ Child's advocate

- ❑ Child-care teacher or provider
- ❑ Chiropractor
- ❑ Clergy, unspecified
- ❑ Clerk, law
- ❑ Clerk, medical
- ❑ Clerk, sales
- ❑ Clerk, unspecified
- ❑ Clothing store owner
- ❑ Coach, life and career
- ❑ Coach, sports
- ❑ Coffee house owner
- ❑ College official
- ❑ College professor
- ❑ Colonic therapist
- ❑ Comedian
- ❑ Computer-aided designer
- ❑ Computer engineer, hardware
- ❑ Computer engineer, networking
- ❑ Computer engineer, software
- ❑ Computer programmer
- ❑ Computer, unspecified
- ❑ Conference coordinator
- ❑ Contractor
- ❑ Convalescent home manager
- ❑ Coordinator, film and television
- ❑ Coordinator, office
- ❑ Coordinator, production
- ❑ Cosmetologist
- ❑ Counselor, licensed marriage and family
- ❑ Counselor, unspecified
- ❑ Court interpreter
- ❑ Court reporter
- ❑ CPR teacher
- ❑ Credit counselor
- ❑ Criminal justice, unspecified
- ❑ Criminal lawyer
- ❑ Criminal psychologist
- ❑ Criminologist
- ❑ Customer relations manager
- ❑ Customer service representative

## D

- ❑ Data analyst
- ❑ Data processor
- ❑ Decorator, film and television
- ❑ Decorator, interior
- ❑ Decorator, store window
- ❑ Decorator, trade show
- ❑ Deli owner
- ❑ Delivery person
- ❑ Dental assistant
- ❑ Dentist
- ❑ Designer, costume
- ❑ Designer, fashion
- ❑ Designer, interior
- ❑ Designer, unspecified
- ❑ Desktop publisher

❑ Die cutter, machinist

❑ Diet counselor

❑ Dietician, registered

❑ Digital audio effects engineer

❑ Digital video effects technician

❑ Disabled person's advocate

❑ Disk jockey

❑ Diver

❑ Document controller

❑ Dog trainer

❑ Doll maker

❑ Drafter, computer-aided

❑ Dressmaker

❑ Driver, unspecified

❑ Drug counselor

❑ Dry cleaner

## E

❑ Earthquake preparedness inspector

❑ Ecologist

❑ Economist

❑ Editor, unspecified

❑ Educational consultant

❑ Educator, unspecified

❑ Electrician

❑ Electronics manufacturer

❑ Electronics salesperson

❑ Embroiderer

❑ Employee benefits specialist

❑ Employee, temporary

❑ Employee's advocate

❑ Employment agency owner

❑ Employment counselor

❑ Employment developer

❑ Employment specialist

❑ Energy conservation advocate

❑ Energy consultant

❑ Engineer, architectural

❑ Engineer, chemical

❑ Engineer, computer

❑ Engineer, electrical

❑ Engineer, hardware

❑ Engineer, mechanical

❑ Engineer, software

❑ Engineer, unspecified

❑ Engraver

❑ Entertainer, unspecified

❑ Entomologist

❑ Environmental consultant

❑ Escort

❑ Escrow officer

❑ Espresso store manager

❑ Espresso store owner

❑ Espresso store worker

❑ Evangelist

❑ Executive coach

❑ Executive director, non-profit

❑ Executive producer, media

❑ Executive recruiter

☐ Executive search consultant
☐ Exercise physiologist
☐ Explorer
☐ Export store owner
☐ Exporter, unspecified

## F

☐ Fabric designer
☐ Fabric store owner
☐ Facilities manager
☐ Farmer
☐ Fashion coach
☐ Fax machine repairer
☐ FBI agent
☐ Feng shui practitioner
☐ Fiber artist
☐ Filmmaker
☐ Financial analyst
☐ Financial consultant
☐ Financial officer, chief
☐ Financial planner
☐ Financial planner, certified
☐ Fire alarm installer
☐ Fire alarm specialist
☐ Fire protection consultant
☐ Firefighter
☐ Fish and game warden
☐ Fish broker
☐ Fisherman or woman
☐ Flight attendant
☐ Flooring contractor
☐ Florist

☐ Flower grower
☐ Food broker
☐ Food buyer
☐ Food manufacturer
☐ Food processing consultant
☐ Food stylist, media
☐ Food supplier
☐ Forest ranger
☐ Freight handler
☐ Freight traffic consultant
☐ Furniture dealer
☐ Furniture designer
☐ Furniture maker

## G

☐ Gambler
☐ Game designer
☐ Gas station owner
☐ Geologist
☐ Geophysicist
☐ Gift manufacturer
☐ Gift shop manager
☐ Glassblower
☐ Gold seller
☐ Golf course architect
☐ Golf shop owner
☐ Golfer, professional
☐ Gourmet chef, professional
☐ Government official, unspecified
☐ Graphic designer
☐ Greenhouse builder

- ❑ Greensman, film and television
- ❑ Greeting card maker
- ❑ Grinder, machinist
- ❑ Grocer
- ❑ Gym manager
- ❑ Gym owner

# H

- ❑ Handyperson
- ❑ Hang-gliding instructor
- ❑ Hardware store owner or manager
- ❑ Health-care practitioner, unspecified
- ❑ Health plan administrator
- ❑ Heating and ventilation specialist
- ❑ Heavy-equipment operator
- ❑ Helicopter pilot
- ❑ Herbologist
- ❑ Historian
- ❑ Holistic healer
- ❑ Horse breeder
- ❑ Horse trainer
- ❑ Horseback riding instructor
- ❑ Horticulturist
- ❑ Hospital administrator
- ❑ Hotel manager or owner, unspecified
- ❑ Human factors/ergonomist
- ❑ Hypnotherapy practitioner, certified

# I

- ❑ Ice cream maker
- ❑ Ichthyologist
- ❑ Illustrator
- ❑ Immigration lawyer
- ❑ Immigration officer
- ❑ Immunologist
- ❑ Importer
- ❑ Income tax preparer
- ❑ Industrial designer
- ❑ Industrial engineer
- ❑ Industrial hygiene consultant
- ❑ Industrial or organizational psychologist
- ❑ Information technologist, unspecified
- ❑ Instructor, unspecified
- ❑ Instrumentation technician
- ❑ Insurance analyst
- ❑ Insurance auditor
- ❑ Insurance claims agent
- ❑ Insurance consultant
- ❑ Insurance salesperson
- ❑ Interior designer
- ❑ Internet access provider
- ❑ Internet consultant
- ❑ Internet game designer
- ❑ Interpreter, deaf
- ❑ Interpreter, multilingual
- ❑ Inventor
- ❑ Investigator, private

❑ Investigator, unspecified
❑ Investor, unspecified

## J

❑ Jeweler
❑ Job development specialist
❑ Job search coach
❑ Journalist
❑ Judge
❑ Juggler

## K

❑ Kennel employee
❑ Kennel owner
❑ Kitchen designer
❑ Kitchen equipment manu-facturer
❑ Kitchen supervisor
❑ Kosher deli owner

## L

❑ Labor advocate
❑ Laboratory assistant
❑ Laboratory technician
❑ Laborer, unspecified
❑ Landscape architect
❑ Lawyer, unspecified
❑ Learning disabilities specialist
❑ Legal assistant
❑ Legislative assistant
❑ Legislator
❑ Librarian

❑ Library employee
❑ Life coach
❑ Lighting designer
❑ Lighting technician, film and media
❑ Limousine driver
❑ Liquor store owner
❑ Literary agent
❑ Literary critic
❑ Lithographer
❑ Livestock rancher
❑ Living trust expert
❑ Loan agent
❑ Locksmith
❑ Logger
❑ Logistics and planning engineer
❑ Logo designer
❑ Lumberyard owner

## M

❑ Machinist
❑ Magazine editor
❑ Magazine publisher
❑ Mail carrier
❑ Maintenance and repair worker
❑ Maintenance technician
❑ Makeup artist, media
❑ Manager, production
❑ Manager, program
❑ Manager, project
❑ Manager, retail

❑ Manager, safety
❑ Manager, stage
❑ Manager, unspecified
❑ Manicurist
❑ Manufacturer, unspecified
❑ Mapmaker
❑ Marine biologist
❑ Marketing analyst
❑ Marketing and communications manager
❑ Marketing and communications specialist
❑ Marketing consultant
❑ Marketing director
❑ Martial arts instructor
❑ Massage therapist
❑ Mechanical engineer
❑ Mediator
❑ Medical assistant
❑ Medical transcriber
❑ Metallurgist
❑ Meteorologist
❑ Midwife
❑ Midwife assistant
❑ Military, unspecified
❑ Mime
❑ Ministorage facility manager
❑ Miniaturist, film and media
❑ Minister
❑ Ministore employee
❑ Ministore owner
❑ Mobile phone customer service representative

❑ Mobile phone salesperson
❑ Model maker
❑ Model, artist's
❑ Model, high fashion
❑ Mortgage broker
❑ Mountaineering guide
❑ Mountaineering instructor
❑ Mounter, photos and pictures
❑ Music producer
❑ Musician, unspecified

# N

❑ Nanny
❑ Narrator
❑ Naturopathic physician
❑ Neon artist
❑ Neurologist
❑ Newscaster, radio and television
❑ Newsletter publisher
❑ Newspaper columnist
❑ Newspaper editor
❑ Newspaper publisher
❑ Newsroom director
❑ Nighttime security guard
❑ Noise control consultant
❑ Notary public
❑ Nuclear scientist
❑ Nurse, certified aide
❑ Nurse, emergency
❑ Nurse, intensive care
❑ Nurse, licensed vocational

❏ Nurse, pediatric
❏ Nurse, psychiatric
❏ Nurse, registered
❏ Nurse, unspecified

# O

❏ Occupational health officer
❏ Occupational therapist
❏ Oceanographer
❏ Office clerk
❏ Office employee, unspecified
❏ Office furniture designer
❏ Office machine technician
❏ Office manager
❏ Office supply store owner
❏ Oil producer
❏ Online customer service representative
❏ Opera singer
❏ Operator, machine, unspecified
❏ Ophthalmologist
❏ Optical engineer
❏ Optician
❏ Optometrist
❏ Optometrist assistant
❏ Oral surgeon
❏ Orchid grower
❏ Organizational development consultant
❏ Organizational psychologist
❏ Ornament maker

❏ Orthodontist
❏ Orthopedic surgeon
❏ Orthotics technician
❏ Osteopathic physician
❏ Outplacement consultant

# P and Q

❏ Painter, buildings
❏ Painter, fine art
❏ Painter, interiors
❏ Painter, sets (theater, media)
❏ Painter, signs
❏ Palm reader
❏ Paralegal
❏ Parapsychologist
❏ Parasitologist
❏ Parole officer
❏ Parts clerk
❏ Pastor
❏ Pastry chef
❏ Patient's advocate
❏ Pattern maker
❏ Payroll clerk
❏ Pediatrician
❏ Perfume maker
❏ Pet store owner
❏ Petsitter
❏ Pharmacist
❏ Pharmacy assistant
❏ Photoengraver
❏ Photofinisher
❏ Photographer

❑ Photography store owner
❑ Physiatrist
❑ Physical therapist
❑ Physical therapy aide
❑ Physical therapy assistant
❑ Pipe fitter
❑ Plant store owner
❑ Plumber, unspecified
❑ Podiatrist
❑ Police officer
❑ Politician
❑ Pollution control technician
❑ Precision die maker
❑ Probation officer
❑ Production manager, film and television
❑ Production manager, industry
❑ Production supervisor, unspecified
❑ Professor, unspecified
❑ Project manager, industry
❑ Prop master, entertainment
❑ Property manager
❑ Property owner, multiple rentals
❑ Psychiatrist
❑ Psychic
❑ Psychoanalyst
❑ Psychologist, educational
❑ Psychologist, unspecified
❑ Psychopharmacologist
❑ Psychotherapist

❑ Public health counselor
❑ Public health officer
❑ Public servant

# R

❑ Racer, professional
❑ Radio announcer
❑ Radio station manager
❑ Radio technician
❑ Radiological technician
❑ Radiologist
❑ Railroad worker, unspecified
❑ Rancher, unspecified
❑ Ranger, forest and parks
❑ Rape counselor
❑ Reader, script
❑ Real estate agent
❑ Real estate assistant
❑ Real estate broker
❑ Real estate investor
❑ Real estate, timeshares
❑ Record store clerk
❑ Record store manager
❑ Records clerk, law
❑ Records clerk, medical
❑ Records clerk, unspecified
❑ Recreation therapist
❑ Recruiter, college
❑ Recruiter, corporate
❑ Recruiter, executive
❑ Recruiter, military
❑ Recruiter, technical

- Referee, sports
- Registered nurse
- Registrar
- Rehabilitation counselor, unspecified
- Repairer, auto
- Repairer, unspecified
- Reporter, news and media
- Researcher, legal
- Researcher, marketing
- Researcher, medical
- Researcher, scientific
- Researcher, unspecified
- Resort groundskeeper
- Respiratory therapist
- Restaurant maitre d'
- Restaurant manager
- Restaurant owner
- Restorer, art and furniture
- Retail clerk, unspecified
- Retail store manager, unspecified
- Retail store owner, unspecified
- Roads and highway worker
- Rubber stamp maker

## S

- Salesperson, unspecified
- Sales consultant
- Scene designer
- School administrator
- School principal

- School psychologist
- Scientist, unspecified
- Screenwriter
- Script supervisor, film and television
- Seamstress
- Security guard
- Seismologist
- Self-employed business owner
- Senior vice president
- Shipping and receiving
- Shoe repairperson
- Shopper, personal
- Shuttle driver
- Singer, opera
- Singer, pop
- Ski instructor
- Social director
- Social psychologist
- Social worker
- Sociobiologist
- Sociologist
- Software designer
- Software engineer
- Software postsales consultant
- Software presales consultant
- Songwriter
- Sound editor
- Sound mixer
- Sound, boom operator
- Sound, Foley artist
- Special effects engineer

❑ Staffing specialist
❑ Store manager
❑ Store owner
❑ Strategic marketing analyst
❑ Stunt performer
❑ Systems analyst

# T

❑ Tailor
❑ Talk show host
❑ Tax return auditor
❑ Tax return preparer
❑ Team leader, unspecified
❑ Technical director, theater
❑ Technical director, television or film
❑ Technical instructor, unspecified
❑ Technician, unspecified
❑ Telecommunications expert
❑ Theologian
❑ Tour operator
❑ Tractor operator
❑ Trainer, unspecified
❑ Travel agent
❑ Travel writer
❑ Tree trimming business owner
❑ Truck driver

# U

❑ Umpire
❑ Underwater researcher
❑ Undertaker

❑ Underwriter
❑ Usher

# V

❑ Vendor
❑ Veterinarian
❑ Veterinary assistant
❑ Vice chancellor
❑ Vice president, unspecified
❑ Visual effects engineer
❑ Voice teacher
❑ Voice-over artist

# W

❑ Waiter or waitress
❑ Warehouse supervisor
❑ Watchmaker or watch repairer
❑ Water aerobics instructor
❑ Wedding consultant
❑ Welder
❑ Wildlife expert
❑ Woodworker

# Y

❑ Youth activities coordinator
❑ Youth drug and alcohol counselor
❑ Youth social worker

# Z

❑ Zookeeper
❑ Zoologist

Great! Now write your 10 top job titles (or titles you added to the above list) here:

1. _____
2. _____
3. _____
4. _____
5. _____
6. _____
7. _____
8. _____
9. _____
10. _____

In the next chapter, you will take the next step and get a detailed view of each of these careers. We're going to do exercises that will give you a feel for the careers you just listed and what it would be like to be doing them.

You'll have the chance to find out the duties, working conditions, qualifications, opportunities, salaries, and more of the 10 jobs you've picked so that, as you narrow the list down to just one career, you are more informed.

You'll also have a chance to imagine yourself (from morning to night) actually doing that job for a day and seeing how it might fit into your entire lifestyle. Most people don't want a job, however rewarding, that consumes their entire life to the exclusion of their health, recreational, spiritual, or family life. Considering other parts of your life in the exercises we're going to do will help you put your new career in perspective and make sure that it's a good fit with your personal life and non–work related goals.

# CHAPTER THREE

# Testing the Waters

You may have found the exercises in the previous chapter challenging. But you completed them, and you should be proud that you've taken those brave steps because there are very few people who take the time to think about what makes them unique. You now have a list of 10 potential jobs that are ideal for you. That means that you're equipped with the knowledge that will help you make a career choice that will be inspiring. Now that you've made the effort to find your talents and your top 10 favorite potential occupations, we're going to see which of those occupations will best suit your needs.

What do I mean by "needs"? All of us have needs for self-expression, economic security, career/life balance, stimulation, relaxation, contribution, and more. It's essential to gauge whether or not, and to what degree, those needs are going to be fulfilled in your occupation so that you're going to truly love what you do.

To determine this, we're going to complete four active exercises together that will help you build a sense of whether or not the job described by that title is *really* right for you.

> **Some of the exercises involve reading and writing while others invite you to actually do or imagine something.**

The four activities are methods of gathering information about you and the job you want. For some, the thought of gathering information may seem daunting or even boring, but I promise it will be fun *and* enlightening.

1. Career Options Research
2. Your Ideal Work-Life Day
3. Your Transferable Skills and Satisfiers Grid
4. The Long View

## *Exercise 1. Career Options Research*

There are two reliable and up-to-date sources you can use to delve into the details about the 10 job titles you've selected. I know of absolutely no better resources for researching careers than these databases to give you a fleshed-out picture of what a particular job might really be like in the real world.

The first source is the O*NET, which is an interactive database that can be found on the Internet and that can be used by anyone at no cost. It is compiled and continually updated by the U.S. Department of Labor. It is an absolutely invaluable tool for career changers because you can search for a job not only by its title but also by its industry and/or the skills needed to do it. You can also explore the fastest-growing jobs, highest-paying jobs, wage and industry trends, and much more on this site. No other source has better quantitative or qualitative information about occupations than this. This gold mine of information can be found at http://online.onetcenter.org.

The second excellent source of information about a wide variety of vocations is the *Occupational Outlook Handbook (OOH)*, which can be found in printed form at your local library, at a college, or community career center. It is published in book form by the U.S. Bureau of Labor Statistics. Basically, it contains much the same information as does the O*NET. Its advantage is that if you don't have access to the Internet for the O*NET, you can find the *OOH* at the library. It's also available on the Internet at no cost at http://www.bls.gov/oco.

Look up each of your 10 career choices on the O*NET and in the *Occupational Outlook Handbook* and take notes that you can refer to later. You're going to be using this information in the rest of this chapter, so pick out what seems important to you and have it readily at hand.

By entering a job title you're interested in, you will find the following:

- A definition of the job and explanation of the responsibilities it entails, down to the smallest details of what the job requires.

- Listings of jobs that are closely related to the title you enter, so that if that occupation isn't right for you, you can view another similar one that may be.

- The usual education, skills, and experience required for breaking into the job.

- Work environments and working conditions.

- Professional organizations that have more information about the occupation.

- Career paths (how one would advance in the career).

- The labor market prospects (the relative ease of breaking in to that position).

- Average range of earnings in the United States. Figures for these salary amounts and forecasts are taken from the Bureau of Labor Statistics. Tabulations for both state and national averages are available.

- A forecast of the job's continuing popularity in the future.

- Work values. (I call these *satisfiers* and we'll be covering this essential component of job satisfaction later in this chapter.)

> *Because having a concrete understanding of what a specific job is like is crucial to knowing how well you'll like it, plan to take a good chunk of your time to really plumb the depths of data on the O\*NET.*

The O\*NET and the *Occupational Outlook Handbook* may not be an *exact* mirror image of you, the job, the requirements, *or the* salary. Instead, they provide a general picture of what the job might really be like. For example, the description may say that a master's degree is *required*, when in fact it is only *preferred*.

---

**Your reference librarian may be able to guide you to other periodicals that cover job market details and salary information calculated for your particular geographic area, usually by county.**

---

After reading carefully about the 10 career choices you select-ed in the last chapter, analyze what you've read, see how it all stacks up, and check with your gut feelings about each profession. As you explore the jobs in the O*NET or the *OOH*, keep asking yourself the question:

To what extent would this occupation allow me to express my authentic calling?

Please take a moment to reflect on and rank each career according to the following criterion: If a career will completely suit your calling, rank it 10. If it is at the bottom of the scale and will not at all fit with your calling, rank it 1.

| *Career Choice* | *Lowest* | | *Highest* |
|---|---|---|---|
| 1. _____ | 1 2 3 4 5 6 7 8 9 10 | | |
| 2. _____ | 1 2 3 4 5 6 7 8 9 10 | | |
| 3. _____ | 1 2 3 4 5 6 7 8 9 10 | | |
| 4. _____ | 1 2 3 4 5 6 7 8 9 10 | | |
| 5. _____ | 1 2 3 4 5 6 7 8 9 10 | | |
| 6. _____ | 1 2 3 4 5 6 7 8 9 10 | | |
| 7. _____ | 1 2 3 4 5 6 7 8 9 10 | | |

| Career Choice | Lowest | Highest |
|---|---|---|
| 8. _____ | 1 2 3 4 5 6 7 8 9 10 | |
| 9. _____ | 1 2 3 4 5 6 7 8 9 10 | |
| 10. _____ | 1 2 3 4 5 6 7 8 9 10 | |

The next step requires you to make a tough choice. Based on the research you've done so far and the list you've compiled above, select just three job titles that sound best to you. If you know of a job title like "pilates instructor" that is not listed in either database, include it as one of your three choices.

1. _____
2. _____
3. _____

Excellent! We'll be exploring these three careers—and how you feel about them—in depth for the rest of this chapter.

## Exercise 2. Your Ideal Work-Life Day

By now you should have a more fleshed-out model of your three job titles. Now it's time to use your imagination to try to understand what these three jobs would be like. For each of the job titles you're exploring, write what a day would be like if you were *really* doing that profession.

On a piece of notebook paper or your computer, describe it in as much detail as possible, using all five senses, from the moment you wake up in the morning to the moment you lay your head down to sleep. Make the day as realistic as possible.

Realistically, who is there when you wake up? What do your bed sheets feel like? What do your bedroom, bathroom, and kitchen look like? What sort of clothes do you put on—sweatpants and a T-shirt, some kind of uniform, jeans and a blazer, or a designer label three-piece suit or dress? What is your jewelry, if any, like? Do you need makeup or not? Do you leave the house or stay in your home to work? Are any children around that you have to get off to school? Do you have a maid or cook? Is a spouse, significant other, or roommate also getting ready for work?

How do you get to work? What kind of car do you drive? Do you have a chauffeur? Is your vehicle racy or practical, an SUV, an economy, or a luxury car? What color is it? How far away, ideally, is your workplace from where you live? Do you work at home? If not, how long is the commute to work? What are you thinking about as you transport yourself to your job? Are you on a train, bus, or subway, or are you walking or riding a bike? Are you listening to music, news, books on tape, learning a foreign language while commuting perhaps, or listening to motivational tapes?

Who is there when you get to work? How do they treat you? Can you imagine something they might say? Are you alone? If not, what is the quality of the interaction between you and others? Do you feel respected, valued, liked, or loved? Imagine what you might be saying to the others. How does your boss, if you have one, interact with you? Are you the boss?

What is the mood? Is it serious or light? Exciting or serene? Chaotic or orderly? Harmonious or tense? Do you feel this company has a sense of integrity? Is is honest? Does it care about its employees? Does it act in a morally upstanding way? Would you feel proud to say you work there? How do you feel about yourself when you are at your place of work doing what you'd ideally like to be doing?

Do you have an office, a cubicle, a workstation, or are you working outdoors? What, exactly, are you doing? Are you primarily using your intellect, your body, your intuition, your emotions, or some combination of all of them?

What do you love about what you are doing? Are you using your gifts? Are you the head of the company, or might you be self-employed? If the company has a hierarchy, where are you on the ladder?

What, exactly, does your place of work look like? Are you in a small, medium, or large company? Does your job require travel? If so, where? Are you in an executive office, at a factory, in a laboratory, at a school, on a movie set, at a hospital, in an airplane, a retail store, or out of doors? Do you work from a car most of the day?

Is your workload heavy, moderate, or light? How many hours do you work in your day? Do you have routine hours and deadlines or flexible time to work at your own pace?

Is it a standard 9-to-5 day, or do you work fewer, different, or more hours? Do you see yourself working at night and/or on call or on the weekends?

---

**What do you most enjoy about this scene? What do you think or feel about yourself as you imagine yourself in this day?**

---

Write a realistic day in your ideal career in as much detail as possible, noticing the feelings and thoughts inside you as well as imagining the environment around you.

Continue in this manner until your workday is over and you return home. What time do you get home, or what time do you stop working? Are you working overtime? How is the commute home? What do you do in the evenings after work and with whom?

How much money do you make in this career? Do you have a comfortable or exorbitant amount of money to spend and invest, or do you have to stay on a more limited budget?

Do you have time for leisure activities? Do you have the energy to run errands or spend some time beautifying your garden? Is there time for a lunch out with a friend, some golf at the driving range, or a game of tennis or racquetball? How about time to go to the gym during lunch or after work? Can you get together with friends at the end of a long day for dinner or drinks? Do you have time to take care of your body and your social and spiritual life? Do you bring work home with you?

With this particular career as part of your day, how do you end your day? Do you share intimacy with someone you love? Do you need to get your children to bed? Do you fall to sleep reading, watching TV, or doing a crossword puzzle? Do you write in a journal or diary?

Maybe you make a list of your goals for the next day or read a good book and end your evening with prayer, contemplation, or meditation. At the end of the evening, do you feel "full" or "empty"?

What time do you go to bed? What thoughts do you have in your mind about your ideal workday as a _____? What feelings do you have about your life and yourself as you reflect back on your day?

Now please write two more realistic days for your other job titles, using the same attention to detail.

When you're finished, you'll have a good idea as to how your three career selections might fit into your everyday life. You'll also have a taste of how your work, home, social, financial, and recreational lifestyle might unfold with each career.

Take a minute and write your notes and observations about each career.

Career 1

_____

_____

_____

Career 2

_____

_____

_____

Career 3

_____

_____

_____

## *Exercise 3. Your Transferable Skills and Satisfiers Grid*

The next key step in creating your career fingerprint is to match your new career to your gifts, transferable skills, and satisfiers. You are unique, and so are your personal preferences. You'll learn about each through the different steps of this exercise.

## Transferable Skills

The first part of this exercise focuses on transferable skills. A *transferable skill* is a skill that can transfer from one job to another. In other words, these are skills you use at your current job that will transfer to whatever profession you choose next. Managing, organizing, and communicating are some of the most common transferable skills because they can be used in such a wide variety of industries and occupations.

Office managers, financial planners, entrepreneurs, and logistics directors are examples of just a few of the careers that entail organizational, management, and communication skills. Although the jobs seem quite different at face value, they share a core group of skills.

Understanding your transferable skills will make it easier for you to change occupations. Your skills go with you. In the next chapter, you'll learn how and why transferable skills are going to be one of the main strategies you'll be using to change careers. For now, focus on learning what your transferable skills are.

This exercise has three steps:

1. On the following list make a checkmark to the left of any of the transferable skills that you already possess, to whatever degree you know how to do them (you don't have to be an expert).
2. Then go back through the list and circle the skills you'd actually like to use in the future. It's okay to circle either checked or unchecked items.
3. Finally, pick six of the circled skills (they don't have to have a checkmark) that you'd really like to use in your next job. Go for it!

## Transferable Skills Checklist

❑ Acting                    ❑ Advising
❑ Advertising               ❑ Aiding

- ❏ Analyzing
- ❏ Arranging
- ❏ Assessing performance
- ❏ Assessing progress
- ❏ Assessing quality
- ❏ Assisting
- ❏ Attending to detail
- ❏ Auditing
- ❏ Budgeting
- ❏ Building cooperation
- ❏ Building credibility
- ❏ Building relationships
- ❏ Building structures
- ❏ Calculating
- ❏ Classifying
- ❏ Client relations
- ❏ Coaching
- ❏ Communicating feelings
- ❏ Communicating ideas
- ❏ Communicating in writing
- ❏ Communicating instructions
- ❏ Communicating nonverbally
- ❏ Communicating verbally
- ❏ Computer literate
- ❏ Conceptualizing
- ❏ Consulting
- ❏ Coordinating
- ❏ Correcting
- ❏ Corresponding
- ❏ Counseling
- ❏ Customer service
- ❏ Dancing
- ❏ Data analysis
- ❏ Data entry
- ❏ Data processing
- ❏ Decision making
- ❏ Decorating
- ❏ Delegating
- ❏ Designing
- ❏ Developing designs
- ❏ Developing systems
- ❏ Developing talent
- ❏ Diagnosing
- ❏ Directing
- ❏ Drafting
- ❏ Drawing
- ❏ Driving
- ❏ Editing
- ❏ Educating
- ❏ Empathizing
- ❏ Enforcing
- ❏ Engineering
- ❏ Evaluating
- ❏ Facilitating
- ❏ Filing
- ❏ Financial planning
- ❏ Forecasting
- ❏ Formulating
- ❏ Fund raising
- ❏ Healing
- ❏ Helping others

❏ Imagining
❏ Implementing
❏ Influencing
❏ Initiating
❏ Intervening
❏ Intuiting
❏ Inventing
❏ Investigating
❏ Leading people
❏ Lecturing
❏ Lifting
❏ Listening
❏ Managing tasks
❏ Marketing
❏ Marketing and communi-
   cations
❏ Massaging
❏ Motivating
❏ Multitasking
❏ Negotiating
❏ Nurturing
❏ Observing
❏ Organizing
❏ Performing
❏ Persuading
❏ Prescribing
❏ Program managing
❏ Programming computers

❏ Project managing
❏ Promoting
❏ Public speaking
❏ Reconstructing
❏ Recording
❏ Repairing
❏ Reporting
❏ Researching
❏ Selling and marketing
❏ Selling
❏ Servicing
❏ Servicing customers
❏ Singing
❏ Supervising
❏ Surveying
❏ Teaching
❏ Team building
❏ Team leading
❏ Telephone skills
❏ Tending
❏ Testing
❏ Tooling
❏ Training
❏ Troubleshooting
❏ Understanding
❏ Using equipment
❏ Writing

My six preferred skills that I'd like to use in the future are:

1. _____

2. _____

3. _____

4. _____

5. _____

6. _____

We'll use this list in conjunction with the next part of this exercise, which is deciding other important career choice factors, which I call your *satisfiers*—that is, the aspects of a job that make it emotionally appealing.

Below is a list of satisfiers. You may find that many or all of these things are important to you; however, I'd like you to carefully focus on the meaning of each of these satisfiers and how they will affect your life *both* in and out of the work setting.

Each of them may sound appealing; however, in this assignment your task is to reflect on which six are the *most* important to you and are the satisfiers that you'd like to have in your next career.

Which of these satisfiers rate as your top six? (Please circle only your top six satisfiers.)

1. A company that is charitable to the community
2. A job that will accommodate my disability
3. A wide range of benefits and/or perks
4. Ample promotion opportunities
5. Beautiful and pleasing surroundings
6. Challenging responsibilities
7. Easy commute
8. Emotional fulfillment
9. Excitement
10. Flexible hours
11. Extremely high income
12. Friendly and respectful colleagues
13. Independence

14. Intellectual challenge
15. Lots of leisure time with family, friends, hobbies, and travel
16. Low stress
17. Possibility for very high earnings and/or commissions and bonuses
18. Power, influence, and authority
19. Routine
20. Spiritual satisfaction
21. Steady income

My top six satisfiers:

1. _____
2. _____
3. _____
4. _____
5. _____
6. _____

## The Transferable Skills and Satisfiers Grid

In the next step in this exercise, you'll combine the information you have gathered so far. It's called the "transferable skills and satisfiers grid." I have adapted it from the work of Howard Figler in the *Complete Job Search Handbook.*

This assignment is exciting because it synthesizes the qualitative information we've gathered in this and the previous chapter and provides a subjective but quantitative look at how the pieces of your career puzzle fit together.

Finally, you'll have information that can influence your choice of one career over the other two, and a starting point to put everything you've learned into action in the following chapters.

1. Make a chart that looks like the one that follows. List your three job titles at the top of the chart. Number the jobs 1, 2, and 3 not in any particular order of preference.

|  | *Job 1* | *Job 2* | *Job 3* |
|---|---|---|---|
| **SKILLS** | | | |
| Skill 1 | | | |
| Skill 2 | | | |
| Skill 3 | | | |
| Skill 4 | | | |
| Skill 5 | | | |
| Skill 6 | | | |
| **SATISFIERS** | | | |
| Satisfier 1 | | | |
| Satisfier 2 | | | |
| Satisfier 3 | | | |
| Satisfier 4 | | | |
| Satisfier 5 | | | |
| Satisfier 6 | | | |
| **GIFTS** | | | |
| Gift | | | |
| Gift | | | |
| Gift | | | |
| Subtotal | | | |
| INTUITION | | | |
| TOTAL | | | |

2. Then list all six of your preferred skills from top to bottom.

3. Next list your six satisfiers.

4. For each of your preferred skills (for example, management), ask yourself, "How well will job 1 satisfy my desire to be a manager?" If it will provide you with an opportunity to be a manager, put a checkmark in the corresponding box. If not, leave it blank.

5. Repeat the same question for each of the other two jobs.

6. Continue using the same methods for all of your skills and satisfiers. For example, "Will job 2 satisfy my need for economic security? Prestige?"

7. Each column should now have several checkmarks. The last step is to look at your gifts.

---

*Because I believe that using your gifts in your career will make you absolutely soar, I'm going to ask that you rate "gifts" on a scale of 1 to 100 for each of the three jobs—for example, "How well will job 1 allow me to express my gifts?" If you have more than one gift, also list them on the chart and rank them from 1 to 100.*

---

8. Now, add all of the checkmarks that appear vertically under job 1 and write your total.

9. Do the same as in step 8 for the other two jobs.

We're not quite finished yet, but stop and take a minute to observe how the totals look. Is one job way ahead? Do others lag behind? Do two or all three have nearly identical scores?

Now, for a final, and most important, indicator, you'll be using your intuition to help you rate these jobs. Please rank each occupation on your chart in terms of your intuitive feeling, from 1 to 100. Again, 100 would mean something like "absolutely fantastic," and 1 would be "horrifying."

What does "intuitive feeling" mean? To some, it may literally be a feeling in the gut, chest, or stomach. Others internally sense some sort of feeling of right or wrong. Others may feel that one choice is simply more clear or rings more true.

This exercise allows you to observe a lot of information at once. Carefully reflect on it. The numbers themselves do not have to decide your career for you, but they are a good indicator of how well you believe a certain occupation will fulfill many of your needs. The chart is only a tool. You must base your decision on what seems best to you. After all, it will be you doing the job, not someone else—not your parents, your spouse, your friend, or me.

## *Exercise 4. The Long View*

Imagine you are near the end of your life, and you are very, very old. As you look back you can see yourself clearly just as you are right now, in the midst of radically changing your course in life. Assume that you have amassed a great deal of wisdom as a result of having a wide array of life experiences—knowledge about yourself, other people, and the way the world works.

Assume also that as you look back at yourself from what I call "the long view," you feel an overwhelming degree of love and compassion for yourself. You may no longer be interested in some of the outer trappings of life—how shiny your new car was, how big your house was, or whether you wore the latest fashions.

With this frame of mind, answer the following questions: *What career would I pick if I were looking with wisdom from the long view? What will make me happy? What can I look back at with a deep sense of pride and sacredness? What career will give me what I really want, deep down inside?*

Enter your discovery here:

_____

_____

_____

Congratulations! You've created your career fingerprint. Whatever career title you chose will be the one that we will use for the rest of the book as you work to quickly change careers. Now you'll see how all of the objective data and self-knowledge you've gathered can be put into *action*, and *fast!*

My No. 1 preferred career is _____.

# CHAPTER FOUR

# *Eight Fast-Track Strategies for Successful Career Changers*

This chapter will introduce you to eight strategies to move you from where you are now to where you want to go. Used one at a time or in combination, these proven strategies will put you on the launching pad for a new career within a few months. Coupled with the goal-setting methods in Chapter 7 and the accelerated job search techniques in Chapter 8, you'll be landed in a new job in less time than you can imagine.

People around the globe have been making swift career changes for years. So . . . just how is it done? I've done extensive firsthand research on some of the most useful actions other people have used to realize rapid career transitions, which I will pass on to you. These strategies, all based on real success stories, are the ones we'll introduce in this chapter and expand upon further in Chapter 6.

Yes, there may be more than eight strategies for career change. Some people inherit a family business or get a foot in the door to a new industry because they already have a friend in that field. Probably the most common model of career change holds that a person must go back to school or receive lengthy training in order to meet the demands of a new position. This is not the method of choice with Fearless Career Change! Of course, if you're aimed at a job that requires by law or by custom that you obtain a long-term advanced degree like an associate's, bachelor's, master's, or doctorate, you may find it more helpful to skip to Chapter 7, where you can begin setting goals for your new career.

> ***For those of you who want to get on the fast track, we're going to hone in on the strategies the majority of my clients have found to be the most successful.***

The eight fearless career change strategies (one or more of which I'd like you to apply) are these:

1. Transferable talents
2. Strategic education
3. On-the-job training
4. Internship
5. Short-term education (90 days or less)
6. Volunteering
7. Just dive in!
8. Entrepreneurship

## Strategy 1. Transferable Talents

A *transferable talent*, as we talked about in previous chapters, is an ability or abilities that can be used in disparate fields. Just as "communication" is a talent that can be used if you're a shoe designer, cashier, or biochemist, a transferable talent is something you can take with you as you move from career to career.

As you will see in the following chapters, a wide range of transferable talents can be used to pave the way to your new career, even if it is an entirely different field or occupation. For example, Miguel used his transferable talent of being facile with numbers when he went from being a mechanical engineer to a personal financial planner. Both fields demand some degree of mathematical talent and experience. The talent of *analysis* could be used in different contexts by a software programmer, doctor, businessperson, or sound engineer.

> ***A multitude of talents are transferable. You might possess several of them without even knowing it. For example, are you a good listener and also good at solving complex problems? These are both talents that can be used in many jobs.***

## Which of Your Skills Might Transfer to Your Dream Career?

Go back to the list entitled "transferable skills," which you completed in the last chapter. Carefully consider how your top six skills might transfer into abilities you might be able to use in your ideal career. Then, take a look at some of the other skills on the list. Do any of them apply to the career you're headed for?

Don't take anything for granted. You might overlook skills like reading, writing, listening, or empathizing, but, after all, people actually do get *paid* to do just those things that, at first glance, seem very ordinary.

> ***Your transferable skills do not just come from your work life.***

Is your sock drawer so neat (even color coded) that some people, if they had access to your sock drawer, might think you're just a little bit "nuts"? It's likely that your skill of being organized could carry over into your authentic calling.

Are you always the friend who offers a shoulder to cry on? Your dream career may utilize these skills: listening, building rapport, empathizing, nurturing, or even giving advice.

Did you ever design a room in your home, draw a map, or compose photographs? Your spatial, coordination, and design skills might be used in scores of different contexts.

Even if the career of your dreams seems to have nothing to do with your last job, transferable skills from your social life, a hobby, schooling, intellectual, or artistic or spiritual pursuits may catapult you into something new and different in your work life.

Some talent that was buried may surface and translate or transfer to a real job in the real world. Sometimes just one skill is needed to bridge the gap to your new pursuit.

Take a moment and think creatively about how one or more of the six preferred skills in the last chapter may be the ones you can rely on or expand upon in a new vocation. If none of the six you picked seem applicable, find one to three others on the list that are applicable and do the following brief exercise.

Skills I can do and that I like, which could be used in my next career are:

1. _____
2. _____
3. _____

## *Strategy 2.  Strategic Education*

*Strategic education* means enrolling in one or more courses in a certificate or degree program and beginning a new job *before* completing the program or simply not completing the degree at all.

For example, Nancy used a wide range of strategies to break into the publishing field. One of those was what I call "strategic education." She enrolled in a copyediting course at a local community college to pick up some new knowledge required in her new field, and before she finished it, a book publishing company hired her.

Community (two-year) colleges do not have complex registration and application procedures. It's just about as convenient for someone who already has another advanced degree to pick up a couple of classes for general interest as it is for someone just getting out of high school to register and declare a major in order to complete an associate's degree.

These colleges are extremely affordable and offer opportunities for young and mature people alike to take one or two classes to brush up on their skills or to earn a certificate in a particular subject like Web design, real estate, physical therapy assistance, marketing, computer networking, computer programming, or early childhood education. These schools also offer two-year associate's (AA or AS) degrees in academic disciplines like psychology, biology, foreign languages, theater and television arts, and art history.

Sometimes their catalogs are sent to households in the areas they serve, or they can be found at places that have other free weekly newspapers and magazines. Otherwise, you can get a hard copy of their semester-long offerings by personally visiting the registrar's office on campus or accessing an electronic catalog online.

As with most education, training, and even seminars that pertain directly to a new or existing business you operate, many costs for education can be deducted from your taxes. It is best to ask your tax professional which courses and programs would be eligible for such a write-off.

---

**The technique of strategic education can also be used to get a promotion within the company you already work for.**

---

It may be that, instead of making a sweeping change to another career altogether, getting a promotion or a new title in the company you already work for will satisfy your needs. Rodrigo, and many other clients I've coached, got promotions just a few weeks after beginning just *one* course in a master's program.

---

**With the benefit of strategic education, you won't have to wait for years to receive a raise and a new title!**

---

Some people who return to school with the intention of completing a degree see their employers reimburse them later for as much as 50 percent of their tuition. You might find that enrolling in just one course is all that your boss needs to see to be convinced that you're really motivated, ambitious, and determined to master new skills.

## Discussing Tuition Reimbursement with Your Boss

If your employer is going to take on part of or all of the expense for your tuition, he or she will want to know whether he or she is making a good investment. Be prepared to show brochures and computer printouts of the typical curriculum from several programs in your area, and plan a discussion with your boss so that he or she feels included in the decision-making process.

It's up to you to make a case for the value, both financially and professionally, of what you'll be gaining by returning to school and in what precise way that will benefit your organization.

Your employer will be much more likely to buy into your course of action if he or she is allowed to bear some of the responsibility of making the decision. Set aside some specially appointed time with your boss to meet and talk about your plans.

To set up a meeting, you might say something like this:

> I've been thinking about pursuing some advanced studies that would *make me more valuable* to our company. I have gathered literature on several of the best programs, and I'd like to have your opinion about them. When can we set up a brief meeting to talk about it?

You can also ask the human resources department whether your company already has a tuition reimbursement program in place. (Many companies do.) If you're working for a smaller company or one without formal tuition reimbursement perks, you might convince your employer to chip in by saying something like this:

> I'd really like to be able to *contribute* more knowledge and take on more *responsibilities* at work. Would you consider covering a percentage of my fees for an advanced degree if I could guarantee that, *in the long run*, my new expertise and training would *save the company money and increase profits?*

You must be creative in thinking about the *concrete* ways that obtaining additional training will affect the employer's *bottom line.* The best way for you to persuade your employer to support your decision to upgrade your education and take a financial interest in assisting you is to *place yourself in your employer's shoes* and ask yourself what changes or improvements in the company would be meaningful from his or her point of view.

For virtually every business, the bottom line has something to do, directly or indirectly, with *making the company profitable and successful.* Think about the following ways you might be able to impact the bottom line at your company:

- Creating or improving products or services that will draw additional revenues for the company
- Helping the company *save time* or money
- Improving the reputation, visibility, and credibility of the company to the public and its customers
- Making a measurable contribution to improving worker morale and productivity
- Decreasing waste, inefficiency, accidents, and downtime
- Troubleshooting problems more effectively and efficiently
- Becoming part of a management team
- Helping the company best the competition

All of the results listed above impact the company's profits in one way or another. When you save time, you also save money. When the company has a more visible presence in the community, it attracts more consumers. If you can improve production or services, you will not only increase customer satisfaction but you may also be able to charge more for those items—again, generating more profits for the business.

When you help your boss connect your proposed educational choice to the kinds of changes or activities that increase revenue, he or she is much more likely to support your decision to seek additional education and quite possibly will supplement your tuition costs.

Present your proposal to receive funding from the company just as you would a formal business presentation. The use of colorful literature from colleges and universities, measurable estimates of the future improvements you expect to make, and the use of visual aids such as charts, graphs, or even simple drawings will all help the employer imagine the possibilities that lay in store for the company if you receive money for additional training.

## Strategy 3.  On-the-Job Training

On-the-job training usually means that you are paid an entry-level salary (or, in some cases, less) for a limited amount of time while you are learning a new profession or trade.

For example, when Scott went from being a customer service representative for a health insurance company to a film and television set dresser, he used the strategy of paid on-the-job training, among others, to facilitate his transition. We'll take a look at exactly how Scott positioned himself to receive this training in the next chapter, as well as examine how other people have used on-the-job training to break into and learn a new occupation.

Some examples of industries that offer on-the-job training are trades (construction, bricklaying, plumbing, manufacturing), fashion, film and television, financial and brokerage firms, all forms of sales, administrative and office work, manufacturing, health and human services, community activism, nonprofit organizations, cooking and fine cuisine, food and beverage, real estate, tourism, travel and cruises, and organizations involved in civic or global environmental, political, health, and education concerns.

One could almost argue that every job involves some sort of on-the-job training, at least enough to get oriented to a new environment, but the industries listed above are the ones most likely to accept inexperienced mature career changers from other fields or students looking for a first-time job.

If you want to find out about businesses that do on-the-job training, it's best to get in touch with an owner or manager of a business and simply ask if he or she, hypothetically, is willing to provide training for a person with little or no experience who also possesses some assets (for example, good problem-solving skills, flexibility, 3.5 grade point average, or a certificate or degree) or any other educational, personal, or professional background that is in your favor. Be careful that the on-the-job training pays you a wage you can live on until you step up to a regular salary.

Be careful: There may be some companies that will try to take advantage of your "trainee" status by extending your training for longer than needed or paying you far less than is reasonable.

For example, a training period that lasts more than a year while paying minimum wage is really not equitable. A two-week to six-month training period with clearly delineated responsibilities, expectations, and supervision and that pays somewhere just about or substantially above minimum wage is a much more reasonable exchange.

When a company offers you on-the-job training, ask who your supervisor will be and what you can expect to learn during the paid training period. Don't let the company use your talents unsupervised and pay you less than it pays other workers to do the same tasks any employee might routinely perform.

---

**Consider asking for an informal written agreement with the employer that states what "milestones" you must master before becoming a full-fledged employee paid at a normal wage.**

---

The agreement can state both what is expected of you as the trainee and what is expected from the employer. It should also clearly state the name or names of your supervisor(s) and the manner in which you will be evaluated at the end of the training period.

More about how, precisely, to target the companies with which you want to form an on-the-job training program and how to get in touch with an owner or manager is outlined in Chapter 8 under the heading "direct contact."

## Strategy 4. Internship

An *internship* (sometimes paid and sometimes unpaid) trades the intern's labor and talent in exchange for his or her learning or advancing in a new occupation. Are internships only for students, right out of high school or college? Absolutely not. I've known people well into their mature years who take advantage of internships. I sought out an internship in career counseling with a government agency in Santa Cruz, California, when I was just starting out as a career coach.

I called the agency, asked for the manager of the career counseling staff, and asked whether or not they had an internship program. After I told her a little bit about myself, she said I could join in on a four-month program in which I would lead workshops for unemployed people. It was an invaluable experience, and though *I didn't receive a lot of formal training*, I got loads of *experience* helping people solve their employment problems to add to my résumé. Just as important, I left with a terrific letter of recommendation on official county government letterhead.

> ***Whether you're volunteering or doing an internship, be sure to ask your employer (usually your immediate supervisor) if he or she would be kind enough to write a recommendation letter. It will benefit you for many years to come.***

Some will say they don't know what to write but would be willing to edit and sign a letter that you write for yourself. This is no time to be modest. Write yourself a stellar letter fit for framing! After all, you've done the work for free.

Han, like Carl, was well into midlife when she sought a certificate in dog obedience training and then completed an internship with a more experienced dog trainer. To set up her internship, she contacted several trainers in her area and told them she had just received a certificate in animal behavior and that she wanted to continue to study her craft under a more seasoned professional.

One of the trainers agreed to let her observe and participate in a "puppy obedience" class. She was able to get a letter of recommendation from the trainer, which she now shows to clients seeking assistance with their pets.

Here is short list of industries that widely accept, and sometimes even depend upon, internships:

- Agriculture
- Animal behavior
- Archaeology
- Counseling
- Dance and art therapy
- Environmental planning and preservation
- Fashion

Name and Title of Supervisor
Name of Business
Business Address
Phone/Fax
E-mail

To whom it may concern:                    June 6, 20xx


It is with pleasure that I write this letter of recommendation for Carl Springer, who was a marketing intern at our firm for two months in spring of 20xx. Mr. Springer performed many of the duties of a regular staff member such as attending staff meetings, working on assignments, and sitting in on presentations to clients. It was with great professionalism, intelligence, and dedication that Mr. Springer took it upon himself to write several pages of new content for our company Web site that are now incorporated into our site.

Although my firm doesn't currently have an opening for a new staff member, I would certainly not hesitate to hire Mr. Springer immediately if it did. In the short time that Mr. Springer was with us, he added a great deal of enthusiasm, team spirit, and innovative marketing ideas. I would highly recommend Mr. Springer to any company seeking a sharp and creative marketing professional.

If you have any questions about Mr. Springer's performance as an intern here at our firm, please feel free to contact me.

Sincerely,


Signature of Supervisor      **(This is mandatory)**
Typed Name and Title of Supervisor

*Sample Letter of Recommendation*

- Fashion design
- Film and television production
- Geriatrics
- High technology
- Manufacturing

- Marine biology
- Mental health services
- Museums
- Printing
- Publishing
- Theater arts

The most valuable resource I can recommend on internship is Mark Oldman's book *Best 109 Internships,* in which he lists scores of companies from the nonprofit, profit, and government sectors.* The list includes such Fortune 500 giants as Hewlett-Packard, Procter and Gamble, and Microsoft as well as unexpected offerings such as MTV, NASA, the CIA, American Conservatory Theater, and even *Rolling Stone* magazine.

The author also indicates that his research shows that 80 percent of companies that hire interns also *pay them well,* even as much as $800 per week.

---

> ***There are ways to maximize the potential of your internship to lead you right into a job, which we'll discuss in Chapter 5.***

---

## Strategy 5. Short-Term Education

*Short-term education,* as I define it, is completing a prescribed program of training in a formal or semiformal setting (such as a school, college, or professional organization) that lasts for 90 days or less.

One of my clients, Carol, made the dive from administrative assistant to midwife assistant in only a few weeks using the strategy of short-term education. Before she received her training, she performed what I call *labor market readiness research.* She called 10 potential employers—midwives, birthing centers, obstetricians—

---

*Mark Oldman, with Samer Hamdeh, *The Best 109 Internships,* 9th ed., Princeton Review/Random House, New York, 2003.

and made sure that the school she had chosen was recognized in the industry, and in her geographic area in particular.

It would be a shame to waste hundreds of dollars, not to mention your time, on a school that did not have a good reputation among employers. The goal of your training is to prepare you to succeed in your new vocation financially as well as professionally.

---

**Labor market readiness research will give you an idea of how willing employers in your area are to hire graduates of your chosen short-term program.**

---

## Steps for Finding Appropriate Short-Term Training Programs

1. Search your local phone company business directory under *schools, training, vocational schools, colleges,* and *universities,* and call the ones that sound appropriate.

   Most community colleges (sometimes called *junior colleges*) have very good short-term certificate programs. Similarly, you will find excellent (and a bit more expensive) certificate programs at university extension and adult education centers.

   If you're unsure about colleges and universities in your area, go to your local library and ask the research librarian to guide you to a resource that will list institutions of higher learning near your home.

   Be sure not to ignore the possibility of studying from your own home computer via distance learning, online learning, and virtual universities.

2. Telephone or set up an appointment with the training center to ask about the following:

   • The length and cost of its program.

   • The content, depth, and breadth of its program.

   • How many years it has been in business, if applicable.

   • Its accreditation, if applicable.

- The credentials of its staff.
- Its job placement rate. (What percentage of graduating students find jobs, and how long does it take them to obtain positions?)
- The average wages for a graduate in his or her first post-training job.
- Opportunities for advancement in the field.
- Information about whether the school fulfills national, state, or local laws and regulations for your new profession, if applicable.
- Telephone numbers of at least three graduates of the program whom you can call.
- Then, repeat the same process as above using your favorite Internet search engine (such as www.google.com or www.askjeeves.com).

3. Experiment, on your chosen search engine, with different ways of saying the same thing (for example, *classes, courses, school, training, program, certification*). Construct a search term (or *search string* of multiple terms) that includes some of the following words:

   1. Name of occupation (for example, *massage therapist, real estate agent,* or *network engineer*).
   2. Type of program (for example, *school, training, certification,* or *license*).
   3. The city, state, or geographic area in which you'd like to study (for example, *Indianapolis, Broward County, Illinois, New York,* or *Nevada*).
   4. If you want to study online, add: *distance learning, online education,* or *virtual universities.*

Some sample Internet search chains are:

- Massage therapist certification Broward County Florida
- Certified life coach online classes
- Certified networking engineer program New Jersey
- Culinary arts certificate Chicago
- Distance learning business administration marketing
- Web design school Seattle

- Fine cabinetry training New Mexico
- Smog technician training Boise
- Dog obedience trainer program Maine

A big part of your homework will be calling former students from the schools or programs that interest you. The dean or owner of the school should, in most cases, be able to provide you with contact information about former students who will be willing to talk to you. When you call the graduates, introduce yourself, state the purpose or your call, and ask these questions:

- Would you recommend the program at that school? If so, why? If not, why not?
- How long did it take you to find a job (or build a business) after graduating?
- How well did the school curriculum prepare you for your new position?
- Are your wages within the range of your expectations? (Do *not* ask them for the amount of money they're earning.)
- Do you enjoy your new career? Why? Why not?
- What is an average day or week like for you?
- Is there anything you would like to change about your job?
- What other advice would you give someone just entering that occupation?

There are many ways to get short-term training for what you want to do. Ellen wanted to become a *certified life coach,* someone who helps people reach personal and professional goals. She searched the Internet for a coaching program she could afford that provided the skills she wanted to master. Ellen followed the steps outlined above and gradually built a successful business for herself.

The school you choose may sound stimulating and fun, but it will only help you professionally if it's acceptable to potential employers. Be sure to do diligent labor market readiness research to determine if your desired future employers recognize and respect credentials from your course of study. We want you to get hired, now!

# *Strategy 6. Volunteering*

Volunteer work is usually less formal than an internship, and, of course, it is unpaid. It means that you donate your labor to a business or organization either for your own philanthropic satisfaction or to learn and practice new skills.

When Nancy went from being a public health administrator to a book editor, she cleverly repositioned herself in the world of publishing by taking a volunteer position as a proofreader at a free weekly entertainment newspaper. Then she was able to combine that experience with the strategic education she also utilized. The result: Nancy had a new job as an editor at a public health book publishing house in less than four months.

Gary became a volunteer at a local public access television station by calling the station manager and asking for an interview. After going through mandatory orientation and training, he became a volunteer camera operator and later went on to work as a professional lighting designer in the television industry.

Becoming a volunteer is much the same process as becoming an intern. Find the person in charge, introduce yourself, briefly state your background and what you'd like to accomplish there, go to an interview, and join the team. You'll not only get a lot of practice (as well as the letter of recommendation) but you'll also begin taking your first steps toward being a professional.

When you're finished with your volunteer position (which can last from just a couple of days to a year or more), you're going to want to get paid for the new skills you've mastered.

---

*It is absolutely acceptable to list a volunteer or internship position just as you would recount a real paying job on your résumé. (See Chapter 8 for sample résumés.)*

---

The preferred way to express that you offered your labor and talents at no charge is not by writing "volunteer" or "intern" as a title on your résumé. If you negotiate a time with your supervisor to talk about a suitable job title to place on your résumé, you can usually upgrade it to something like *associate, assistant, coordinator, specialist,* and in some cases of more advanced work, *consultant.*

For example, Carl, our marketing intern, might fashion an agreement with his employer to list the time he spent there as *marketing associate* rather than *intern*. Gary, who volunteered at a TV station, might negotiate with the station manager for a title like *camera operator* rather than *volunteer*. Here are some titles for volunteer and internship positions that may be appropriate for a résumé:

- Assistant to the director
- Associate instructor
- Biochemist associate
- Customer service associate
- Executive or personal assistant
- Fashion technologist
- Financial consultant
- Human resources assistant
- Laboratory technician
- Networking assistant
- Property management assistant
- Public relations coordinator
- Software consultant
- Technology specialist

## *Strategy 7. Just Dive In!*

Sometimes a career change does not require special study, training, or strategy. There are instances when all that's required is guts. I call this method *Just Dive In!* For example, Rita, who was "between jobs" and working as a house cleaner, took the plunge when she submitted her first work of fiction for publication. Once she took that risk, she began submitting her work to a myriad of publication sources, and finally, she wrote two books that were handled by a major publisher.

In another instance of Just Dive In! is Jennifer, an interior designer, who came upon a way she thought women could gain control of their finances. She had a hunch that the method she discovered might work.

Without any qualifications (other than managing her own finances with this method), she put a tiny classified ad in the newspaper that advertised a six-week class and support group for women who wanted to become more financially stable, for which she would be the group leader.

She charged $10 per person for six weeks and held the meetings in her home. It worked! Soon she went from teaching one class a week to three. Years later, Jennifer's work is known around the United States. She appeared on major talk shows and she wrote several books. The current cost of a one-day seminar with her? $450.

Just diving in is not for everyone. It is really for people who feel they have a knack for something and don't want to go through an educational process to begin to do that something for a living. The notion to take steps forward into the unknown may emerge as just a hunch that may not seem at all logical to an outside observer.

> *Following that hunch may involve taking risks and even bearing ridicule from people who may be concerned for your welfare but do not share your vision.*

That said, just diving in takes high levels of self-esteem; a willingness to fail as well as prevail: the ability to tolerate uncertainty; a love for improvisation or thinking on your feet; and the ability to learn from mistakes. Jobs that absolutely require some sort of previous experience and have laws regarding certification, like registered securities trader, are not conducive to this strategy. Other types of industries, though, like the arts, hospitality, retail, senior services, community health and improvement services, entertainment, consulting, any type of sales, public speaking, home crafts and repairs, holistic healing, and travel are good bets if you're planning to Just Dive In.

You are especially valuable in the social services such as health, welfare, and education if you speak one or more languages in addition to English, or your native tongue.

Many government agencies like the county public health department, the state department of rehabilitation, and public libraries, will forgo both educational credentials *and* experience if you are fluent in Spanish, Farsi, Vietnamese, Russian, Chinese, French, Arabic, Afrikaans, Italian, or other languages spoken by part of the populace in your community.

---

**If you feel like you can Just Do It and "it" does not legally or ethically require that you have a special license, degree, or designation, then most probably you can move forward to whatever "calls" to you, as long as you're willing to take the ride of your life!**

---

People who use the strategy of just diving in tend to hurl themselves forward headfirst and usually enjoy learning to swim. In fact, they get an incredible *thrill* out of taking just this kind of challenge. If you think you're this type of person, you probably have an *intuition or intense inner feeling* telling you to go ahead. *I invite you to do it!*

## Strategy 8. Entrepreneurship

An *entrepreneur* is someone who initiates and usually (but not always) runs his or her own business.

Ever thought you could go from being an administrative assistant to a CEO in one day? All you have to do is open your own business and put your own name at the top of the organizational chart. Alice's entrepreneurial story in Chapter 6 will tell you how she did it.

Later, in Chapter 9, we'll highlight, in detail, how you can go about making the path of entrepreneurship work for you. You'll be taking a self-assessment that will help you highlight the strengths you bring to your new enterprise as well as the areas that need improvement.

By seeking out supplemental skills or the advice of other experts and professionals, you'll be better equipped to turn your new venture into a successful one. In the chapter on entrepreneurship, you'll also learn about *just how motivated you are* to weather the ups and downs of running your own business. Resources will be offered pertaining to how to take full advantage of the ample financial and professional support available from the government for which you are, most likely, eligible. You'll even get a taste for writing a marketing and business plan.

## Combining Fearless Career Change Strategies for Maximum Impact

Although we've considered each of the strategies on its own thus far, the fastest results tend to arise from combining two or more of the approaches. For example, you might take a short-term series of courses *and* volunteer in your new field, to make your credentials and expertise that much more attractive to your new employer.

Blending strategic education with a well-aimed internship could even land you a *permanent* job at the organization for which you're an intern. An entrepreneur who takes some business classes to augment his or her transferable skills is likely to be that much more well rounded in executing his or her new endeavor.

One of my clients combined strategic education (enrollment in a graduate course), short-term education (a certificate earned by attending a number of seminars), an internship at a well-respected institution, and volunteering for a community group when he made his radical career change.

Which strategies you choose to utilize depends upon the money and time you wish to invest, the requirements of your new position in the real-world marketplace, and just how much of a foundation you wish to lay out before launching your new career. A good deal will also depend on your ability and willingness to take risks—to just dive in.

You must be curious about the details of many of the stories and concepts touched on in this chapter. In Chapter 6, you'll get blow-by-blow accounts of how real people transformed their special calling into a way of life.

# CHAPTER FIVE

# Strategic Education

## What Is Strategic Education?

In the previous chapter, we examined, firsthand, the tremendous benefits career changers receive from utilizing strategic education. Once again, *strategic education* means enrolling in a certificate or college degree program without necessarily having the intention to finish that program.

***Of course, you might want to finish the whole program, but strategic education means that by simply being enrolled in the program and taking one or two classes, the employer will perceive you as already having a certificate or a degree.***

This strategy has worked time and again for thousands of people. The reason it is so effective for career changers is that it focuses on your *future*—the *intent* of where you're going—rather than your past. When the employer perceives *where you are going*, he or she sees several positive qualities in you.

> **Ambition, drive, motivation, and willingness to learn are only a few of the positive connotations the employer infers from the fact that you are trying to better yourself and improve your knowledge through enrollment in a training or education program.**

## You May Be Eligible for Government-Funded Retraining

If you have been laid off in the last 16 weeks (note that the time limit may vary from state to state), the local office of your state's *employment development department* (EDD) may be able to assist you with payment for your entire certificate program. It is doubtful that the EDD will fund a degree program, but it is quite common for someone who has recently been downsized to be able to receive funding up to $10,000 for up to nine months of classes in a certificate program.

> **It is important to note that there is a window of time within which you must inform the EDD that you wish to be considered for a retraining program.**

In the state of California, for example, you cannot enroll in any of these programs using government funding past the 16-week mark of your first unemployment claim. In other words, the faster you communicate your desire to get retraining after being laid off, the better.

If you wait until after the enrollment period, you will not be eligible for government assistance in retraining. It is also important to note that you must make a case for retraining.

There must be some *reason* that you cannot return to your normal occupation. Some of these reasons could be that the job market is too slow in your former occupation, that you have some disability that prevents you from going back to your old profession, or that you need additional education to be competitive in your former career.

You also have to *prove* that the new occupation you are seeking is appropriate for you and is likely to result in your getting a job or being successful in your own business. You can do this by cutting out newspaper ads or by printing a job description from the Internet and showing how they indicate your need for additional education.

## How to Find "Open" Certificate and Degree Programs

You don't have to be laid off to take advantage of the certificate programs listed in this chapter. You need only contact community colleges, vocational schools, adult education programs, or continuing education programs in your region to find many of these programs. You can also research your educational choices on the Internet.

Even though the money will be coming out of your own pocket, remember that you are not necessarily paying for the entire certificate or degree program. You may be paying for only one class as a way to catapult yourself into a new category wherein you are more employable in the new career of your choice.

Another way to utilize strategic education is to enroll at a college or university in a program of study leading to an associate's degree (usually two years), a bachelor's degree (usually four years), a master's degree (usually two additional years from the bachelor's degree), or a PhD program (which sometimes requires a bachelor's and other times requires a master's degree for entrance).

Normally, many schools require that you provide them with extensive documentation before entrance into one of these degree programs. The documentation may include a detailed application with an application fee, letters of recommendation, references, an essay, or written testing.

There is, however, a way to enter colleges and universities strategically by choosing institutions that offer open enrollment, open university, or adult education courses, which do not require these documents at all. You might also find a university on the Internet with online distance learning that has the equivalent of open university. Just be sure that the university is legitimate, accredited, and reputable.

A legitimate institution should provide you with a list of its accreditations before you spend your time and money. Make sure

Most of these are certificate programs run by university extension programs or private vocational schools. This list is not inclusive of, nor is it a guarantee of, all programs that may exist in your local area.

- Accounting and/or bookkeeping
- Administrative assistant
- Air transportation worker
- Alcohol and drug counseling
- Architectural design
- Automotive repair
- Back office medical assisting
- Bioinformatics
- Biotechnology
- Business administration
- Business administration, emphasis in finance
- Business analyst
- C language programming
- Career coaching
- Career planning
- Certificate in computer and information science
- Certificate in e-commerce management
- Cisco-certified engineer
- Clinical design
- College admissions
- Computer-aided drafting
- Computer application developer
- Computer graphics
- Computer network support
- Computer programming
- Computer service technician, A+ certification
- Construction inspector
- Construction manager
- Data entry
- Data warehousing
- Database management systems
- Database specialist
- Dental lab technician and assistant
- Digital signal processing
- Early childhood education
- Earthquake engineering
- E-commerce engineering

*Sample of Some Government-Funded Training Programs*

- Educational therapy
- Entrepreneurial management certificate
- Environmental education
- Environmental health and safety
- Event and meeting planner
- Facilities management
- Fine arts
- Garden design
- Graphic design
- Hazardous materials management
- Heating and air-conditioning technician
- Holistic health practitioner
- Human resource management certificate
- Interactive media
- Interior architecture
- Interior design assistant
- International business
- Internet security
- Java programming
- Landscape architecture
- Linux system administration
- Local area network (LAN) administrator
- Management of Internet technology
- Marketing
- Marketing and communications certificate
- Massage therapist
- Mechanical design
- Medical front office
- Microsoft-certified systems engineer
- Net development
- Network engineering
- Nonprofit management
- Object-oriented programming
- Occupational safety and health management
- Office management
- Oracle database administrator
- Pharmacy technician
- Photography
- Professional personal coach
- Program and project management certificate
- Public relations
- Purchasing management certificate

*Sample of Some Government-Funded Training Programs (Continued)*

- Semiconductor technology
- Senior human resource management certificate
- Senior marketing and communications certificate
- Software engineering
- Teaching English as a second language
- Technical writing
- Telecommunications engineering
- Telecommunications technician specialist
- Training and development
- UNIX system management
- Web master
- Web page pesigner
- Wireless communications
- Word processing

*Sample of Some Government-Funded Training Programs (Continued)*

that the accreditation is applicable to your geographic area, and that, if you are going to complete a degree in something that requires a license in your state, such as marriage and family counseling, or nursing, the college is approved by your local licensing board.

A single class may cost from $50 in the community college up to $1,100 at a university. It isn't possible to fit in this chapter or even in this book the multitudes of institutions of higher learning that offer this type of open enrollment. The best course of action is to call the colleges and universities in your area and find out whether they offer open enrollment or open university and whether or not they have a degree program in something you're interested in that would apply directly as a qualification for your new profession.

> ***Try starting with your own state university program. Government-sponsored universities are always properly accredited and may be the most likely to have an open-door policy.***

When you find one of these programs, it is very likely that all you will need to sign up for it will be your social security number, credit card, name, and phone number. With that, you should be able to start studying within a month or two, if not weeks or days.

If you take more than two or three classes, most of these colleges or universities will require that you fill in the documentation and formally apply for entrance into the degree program. The two or three classes that you have taken up to that point will, most likely, apply to the credits needed for the degree.

---

> ***In the next chapter, you'll meet several people who were actually hired for a new position while they were still taking their first class.***

---

## *Changing Your Résumé*

How can you let the employer know that you're involved at an institution of higher learning? Clearly your strategic education is something you want to emphasize so that it stands out on your résumé. In Chapter 8, we'll discuss using summary statements in your résumé. Add that you are enrolled in a program in this paragraph by saying:

> Currently enrolled in the course of study leading to a _____
> degree in _____ at the University of _____.

If you feel uncomfortable saying "a course of study leading to a degree," you can alternatively use one of these statements:

1. Currently enrolled in undergraduate courses in _____ at _____ College.
2. Currently enrolled in graduate courses in _____ at _____ Institute.

In those first few crucial seconds as the employer reads your résumé, he or she will know that you are making the effort to increase your knowledge through education and will be duly impressed by your *intent to learn.* That's the beauty of strategic education!

*CHAPTER SIX*

---

# *Ten Success Stories About People Just Like You*

---

In the 10 stories to follow you'll be able to easily identify the fear-less career change strategies presented in the last chapter. Don't try to memorize them all. Just watch the stories unfold and see if you find any strategies you like or any *strategy that would best fit* your individual situation. Keep in mind that it is rare to use just one strategy alone. If you're planning to make a career change as rapidly as these people did, it's possible that you may use two or more strategies to reach your goal.

---

> **The people in this chapter may have combined as many as three or four strategies to transport themselves into the new enterprise as quickly and inexpensively as possible.**

---

Fear is normal. Stepping up in spite of fear is exceptional. In this chapter, you'll see how other people overcame the anxiety that sometimes accompanies change and transformed the energy of anxiety into action. When you use these strategies, you too will have the power to instigate and complete your transition successfully. No matter how easy the changes these people made may seem, there is almost always an element of risk involved in a career change. But remember, you've handled risks before.

---

***All risks are double edged. On one hand, they can be frightening, but on the other hand, calculated risks can lead to terrific triumphs.***

---

All of the following stories are true, almost to the letter, except for the names of the people and the companies they worked for. These individuals are not different—not more courageous, conscientious, or clever—from you. The only difference is that they took *decisive action in spite of fear and unpredictability,* and they succeeded. Let's review these 10 people's stories and see what can be learned from them.

# Fearless Career Changers

## From Landscaper to Environmental Planner in Four Weeks Using Strategic Education

**Name:** Marie

**Former occupation:** Landscaper

**New occupation:** Environmental planner

**Primary strategy:** Strategic education

**Other strategies:** Transferable talents, on-the-job training

**Length of time from career decision to a paid position:** One month

**Cost (if any) of transition:** $350

At 38 years old and working as the head of her own landscaping company, Marie had plenty of compelling reasons to want to change her profession. "First," she said, "my body isn't holding up to the strain of bending, lifting, and crawling day by day. My wrists are getting tendonitis from working in rocky soil. I'm tired of running my own business, and I'd like to get on someone else's payroll." She didn't need to provide other reasons, but she did. She also expressed that she wanted more intellectual stimulation, more positive impact on the natural environment, and, in her words, more "recognition" that she believed she could get from a more "prestigious" job.

---

*Admitting that you want more power, prestige, or recognition may be considered unpopular in some circles, but it's your career and your life. In the Fearless Career Change philosophy, it's fine to want these things. But you can get them only if you first admit to yourself that you want them and then go about fashioning a career that will maximize your chances of getting those satisfiers met.*

---

Marie had received a BS in biology from Yale University. Before we met, she had made several attempts to break into the field of environmental planning, without success. She related that employers gave her the feedback that she was academically lacking for the position. Even though she had a bachelor's degree from one of the most prestigious schools in the United States, they could not accept her application without a master's degree. Environmental planning, she felt, would utilize the talents she already had and give her a hand at making a real impact on conserving and restoring the earth's natural environment. She felt at a loss because she didn't feel she had the time to attend graduate classes for two years or more. She especially didn't want to spend "another minute" running her own business.

Since she wanted the transition to be quick, she decided to use the fearless career change plan for strategic education. She called a local university and found out that it had a program called "Open University" in which students could enroll immediately without submitting transcripts, essays, or letters of recommendation.

The only things she needed to register were her driver's license and her social security number. When she checked the catalog for an appropriate course, she found that the university offered a master's program in environmental planning—exactly what she was looking for!

She would be allowed to take up to six units (two semesters) on an open-university basis (without formally being accepted into the degree program), which could then be applied to her master's degree in environmental planning, should she choose to go ahead with the completion of the degree. After six units, she would be asked to apply in the traditional way (with transcripts, an essay, and letters of recommendation) to the master's program.

---

**If you are planning to use strategic education, be sure to check with several universities—whether local or online—to see what their policies are on open enrollment.**

---

If you're looking for classes that could be applied to an advanced degree program, look under *open university, continuing education, open enrollment,* or *adult education* at the institution of your choice. If you'd like to find a university or college that offers open enrollment in your town, try a series of search strings on a good Internet search engine like google.com or www.aol.com that include the words (whichever are appropriate for you) *open enrollment university Boston.*

For example, the search string *open university online marketing* yields Web addresses for dozens of schools. Also, *open enrollment masters degree Chicago* shows multiple offerings at universities as well as online. You might try *continuing education computer networking Miami* and find that you have several choices to investigate.

Even something as unusual as *museum curator degree open enrollment* yields some interesting results.

---

**As you can see, it's important to try several different ways of entering your search strings. You must experiment with many ways of saying the same thing.**

---

If *open university* doesn't work for the subject that interests you, *continuing education* or *adult education* might. If *museum curator* isn't producing the results you want, *art historian* may. You may find nothing that catches your eye when you enter the word *psychology*, but discover a number of offerings if you call it *counseling*.

You'll surely come up with some degree programs that will allow you to take a limited number of classes without undergoing the time and paperwork of the regular admissions process.

Marie paid $350 for her first graduate course and attended class just one night per week. By about the second week, she tried changing the summary clause of her résumé (which you'll learn about, in detail, in Chapter 8) to include the phrase *currently enrolled in a course of study leading to a master's degree in environmental planning at California State University at Hayward.*

By specifying on her résumé that she was enrolled in a relevant graduate course, Marie immediately got interviews with three environmental planning companies that had formerly rejected her. Before she ever made it to her third week of class, Marie had *two job offers!*

---

**Why did strategic education make all the difference? Because her potential employers were more interested in her intent, that is, where she was going, than where she had been before.**

---

Marie finished the course but never completed the master's degree. She started her first day only weeks after registering in the class. She was helping a team of scientists clean up the swamplands on the Northern California coastline. The last time I talked to Marie, she was working for the state of California, tagging baby owls for a scientific study. "I love what I'm doing," she said, "and my salary is three times what it was when I was a landscaper."

---

**This story may sound too good to be true, but this is exactly how it happened. You'll hear several more accounts of just how powerful strategic education can be as this chapter unfolds.**

---

Let's review the fearless career change strategies Marie used to propel her through her swift transition:

| | | | |
|---|---|---|---|
| 1. Transferable talents | *Yes* | Knowledge of plants, soils, and plant ecosystems. | |
| 2. On-the-job training | *Yes* | Marie had to learn more about animal ecosystems by using a combination of continued informal study and absorbing what she could through her work experience. | |
| 3. Strategic education | *Yes* | Partial grad. Course in environmental planning. | |
| 4. Short-term education | No | | |
| 5. Internship | No | | |
| 6. Volunteering | No | | |
| 7. Just Dive In! | No | | |
| 8. Entrepreneurship | No | | |

## From Mechanical Engineer to Financial Advisor in Seven Days Using Short-Term Education

**Name:** Miguel

**Former occupation:** Mechanical engineering project manager

**New occupation:** Personal financial advisor

**Primary strategy:** Short-term education

**Other strategies:** On-the-job training

**Length of time from career decision to a paid position:** Seven days

**Cost (if any) of transition:** $0.00

Miguel, who worked as a project manager in the engineering department of a Fortune 500 company, was laid off over a year ago and came to me for career coaching at the persistent urging of his wife, who, he confided, was "tired of seeing him jump from engineering job to engineering job," only to be laid off again and again due to the massive flux in that industry.

Miguel too was not pleased about being a pawn to a poor economy, but he said that he felt "insecure" about changing careers midstream, saying, "I cannot see changing careers at this point in my life. I worked for six years to get my MSEE (master's in electrical engineering) and my salary is—or was—the highest it has ever been in my life."

It was not until completing the career fingerprinting process that Miguel began to think that there might be something more for him in a different field.

> *Though he was fearful about leaving the familiar territory of high technology, the power of his true calling proved to have the thrust to override most of his trepidation.*

Miguel's unique calling turned out to be "teaching, advising and mentoring others so that they can reach their full potential." With this newfound self-knowledge, he began to cautiously consider some positions other than engineering that might fulfill his love of guiding and advising others. Miguel chose to research the positions of postsales engineering, architecture, and certified financial planning and submitted them to comparison.

He found out a lot about financial advising that attracted him. Number 1 was the intensive contact with people and the opportunity to act as a counselor and mentor to those wishing to achieve their full financial potential. The second feature of the new position that caught his eye was the almost unlimited amount of money that can be made by a financial advisor, as he would be paid a base salary plus bonuses and commissions.

Although the first year or so as a financial advisor can be challenging, while you are building a client base, later years (as early as the third, according to his research) can yield up to $375,000 and more.

Miguel had to admit that sounded good. Two ski trips a year, two new cars, a new house, retirement investments, and a vacation house in Florida were all part of a lifestyle he and his wife had dreamed about. If he could potentially have all this and *work with people* almost 75 percent of the time, he would certainly thrive!

When Miguel made up his mind about changing directions, he called several of the major finance and brokerage companies in his area to see if any of them had training programs for new brokers. One, a Fortune 500 company, brought him in for interviews and testing and then offered him a spot in their 12-week training program.

Although he was paid only minimum wage to complete the training program (as was everyone), his wife's salary as a social worker was more than enough for them to get by for a few months. When he finished the course, he took a state-administered licensing exam to become qualified to sell various financial services. He was then formally offered the position.

Miguel reports that he has loved his first year at the job. "It's really about helping people reach their full potential. Once they take control of their finances, their whole lives turn around. I love being part of that." Miguel was able to use his transferable talents of teaching and advising from his last job as a project manager and his math skills from engineering.

Most important, Miguel tells me that he is living up to his *own* potential and purpose—and getting a lot better at skiing.

To sum up, let's take a closer look at Miguel's use of the fearless career change strategies:

| | | |
|---|---|---|
| 1. Transferable talents | *Yes* | Math and people skills. |
| 2. On-the-job training | *Yes* | First year of job involved closely supervised training. Miguel was given a mentor at work with whom he studied sales techniques for several hours a day. |
| 3. Strategic education | No | |
| 4. Short-term education | *Yes* | 12-week intensive paid training program |
| 5. Internship | No | |
| 6. Volunteering | No | |
| 7. Just Dive In! | No | |
| 8. Entrepreneurship | No | |

## From Public Health Educator to Book Editor in Three Months Using Volunteering

**Name:** Nancy

**Former occupation:** Public health administrator

**New occupation:** Book editor

**Primary strategy:** Volunteering

**Other strategies:** Transferable skills, strategic education

**Length of time from career decision to a paid position:** Three months

**Cost (if any) of transition:** $150.00

Nancy was a high-level public administrator who had a master's degree in public health and PhD in sociology. Just after completing her degree in public health, she joined the county health department of a U.S. eastern seaboard town. Over a 12-year period, Nancy worked hard to focus her efforts on becoming the director of public health for her county. It was after her third year as director that she felt the stirrings of the need for a change. "I don't know what's wrong," she said. "I'm at the top of my field, at the top of the salary range, and yet, I feel like something's missing."

She continued, "I don't feel like going to work in the morning anymore. I feel distracted and frustrated. I can't figure out why I just don't like my job anymore. Since I have such a coveted position and I make such a good living, I almost feel like I don't have a right to complain. Most people would give anything to be in my position."

Many people like Nancy become educated in a field that interests them when they're in their twenties or thirties, but their needs and tastes change with the arrival of another decade. There is certainly no law, written or unwritten, that says just because you were *once* content with a job and did it well, that you can't change your mind. Career interests can change just as the rest of you changes—emotionally, spiritually, intellectually, and so on.

> *The key is that you are not most people. It's your career, your day, your life that you have to reckon with at the end of the day—not someone else's opinion of the ideal job.*

It was evident to Nancy that she needed a change. She didn't need a reason. Her desire to change was all the reason she needed. She told me that she felt somewhat "guilty" about leaving a career she had worked so hard to build and afraid to leave such a "sure thing." Yet, she reflected, "I feel like I'm going to stagnate and die if I continue on in this way."

In spite of her malaise, Nancy still had a few moments of enjoyment in her job. She thought about it and said that she really loved writing and editing reports. "If that were *all* I were doing," she said, "I would be completely content!"

When Nancy completed the career fingerprinting process, she realized that, indeed, her authentic calling involved writing and editing. "I don't know how I didn't see that before. All through school, and throughout my life, that is where I've felt most comfortable and the most challenged."

Nancy researched the positions of journalist, technical writer, and book editor. She concluded that a career as a book editor felt like a good fit. It would be a big change, but she already had polished transferable talents in writing and editing that would ease her transition.

She knew she would need to start near the middle of the ladder in the publishing arena, but with her education and intelligence she would easily rise to the level of editor, and even higher. Volunteering and strategic education turned out to be her recipe for a successful transition.

First, she volunteered to work at a free local newspaper that would publish some of her own writing so that she could start building a portfolio (some call it a *clip sheet*) of her work. She also was able to get some proofreading experience there. Small, underfunded newspapers are often glad to have someone offer to work for free. She got two of her own articles into print—not a bad start!

Though she was still working at her old job, her mood improved dramatically. "I'm having fun again. This feels like play!" By building a bit of a reputation at a small level, Nancy was able to get letters of recommendation from the editor-in-chief and the publisher of the weekly newspaper.

> *Letters of recommendation after a period of volunteering or an internship are an absolute necessity if you're going to use either strategy in your fearless career change arsenal.*

The second line of attack turned out to be strategic education. She enrolled in a semester-long class in what is called *copyediting.* Copyediting is similar to proofreading, also using a specialized group of characters and symbols to make corrections to the text on a page.

Before Nancy finished the course, she had a job offer for an associate editing position in a small educational publishing house. (We'll talk about how she was able to get an interview in Chapter 8.)

About three years later, with two promotions under her belt, Nancy and her family have traded in the cold rocky coast of Rhode Island for a telecommuting job from Santa Fe, New Mexico. Nancy does her editing, and some writing, from her computer at her desk in her desert home and still works, by fax, mail, and e-mail, for her original publishing company. When she sits out on her hardwood deck with her laptop and a cup of coffee overlooking the contours of a desert landscape, she e-mails me a simple message, "Life is good."

For a quick review of Nancy's fearless career change strategies, consider the chart below:

| | | |
|---|---|---|
| 1. Transferable talents | *Yes* | Writing and editing from school and work. |
| 2. On-the-job training | No | |
| 3. Strategic education | *Yes* | Partial course in copyediting. |
| 4. Short-term education | No | |
| 5. Internship | No | |
| 6. Volunteering | *Yes* | Proofreader at a local newspaper. |
| 7. Just Dive In! | No | |
| 8. Entrepreneurship | No | |

## From Customer Service Representative to Film Production Assistant in One Day Using On-the-Job Training

**Name:** Scott

**Former occupation:** Insurance company customer service representative

**New occupation:** Film production assistant (explained below)

**Primary strategy:** On-the-job training

**Other strategies:** Just Dive In!

**Length of time from career decision to a paid position:** One day

**Cost (if any) of transition:** $0.00

Scott was one of my students in a two-day career transition seminar in Northern California. He was working as a customer service representative for a prominent health insurance organization. Scott was laid off from his job there due to massive downsizing because of budget cuts in the company.

Scott told me at the beginning of the workshop that he would like to do "just about anything" other than work in customer service for his next career. "The customers are rude. I have to meet a daily, weekly, and monthly quota, and I'm just not cut out for this kind of work."

In the seminar, Scott had the opportunity to examine just what kind of work he *was* cut out for. He had just "fallen into" working in the insurance industry to pay the bills while he finished college. After he graduated, he just stayed in a groove (or perhaps, as he might later characterize it, a rut). He had been working for the insurance company for three years. The pay was good. The commute was short, and he was a friendly sort who enjoyed his coworkers.

His authentic calling was not at all far from the surface. He had majored in art in college with the hopes of breaking into the film industry as an art director, but he had been sidetracked in the process by the illusive security of his customer service position.

If he wanted to break into the film industry at this point, he could utilize transferable skills like aptitude for color and design and for working with paint, clay, and other media to help ease his way into a lower-rung position and then work his way up to a department head.

In film, perhaps more than any other industry (except perhaps the military), it is necessary to work your way up the ladder, one rung of responsibility to the next, if you are going to be the head of a department. You may, indeed (as the cliché goes), be getting coffee for the boss on the first day out, even if you have a master's degree.

> **It is the finesse and enthusiasm with which you do the rote (and often boring or unattractive) tasks involved in an entry-level position in just about any industry that will get you noticed by a person who may have the power to promote you.**

Scott used his local chamber of commerce to find a movie that had just started filming in his town. Since the chamber had the phone number of the production coordinator, he was able to call and get the name of the hiring manager—in this case, the art director.

The chamber of commerce has information about *all* of its corporate members, and most reputable businesspeople and companies from diverse industries join the chamber. You'll find information on everything from golf teachers to semiconductor manufacturers at the chamber, and its staff will be characteristically helpful about assisting you with your inquiries.

He used a technique called *direct contact* (which you'll learn how to master in Chapter 8) and called his way directly to the art director who was involved, at that very moment, on the set of the film. He then presented his phone script (an easy summation of your skills that you'll write in Chapter 8).

> Hello. My name is Scott R. I have a bachelor's degree in art. I am excellent with people, and I would be glad to show you my design portfolio. Last year, I built sets for two community theater productions, and I have excellent references from the directors. When can I come in for an interview?

"Do you have a truck?" was the only interview question asked by the art director. "As a matter of fact, I do," Scott said.

He was hired *on the phone* and asked to show up at 7:45 the next morning. Scott didn't just get lucky. He was able to effectively communicate his transferable skills to the employer, and he was willing to take the risk of just diving in, relying on his own ability to improvise, learn quickly, and adapt to new situations. He also accepted the fact that he'd have to initially work at entry level and learn everything he could through direct on-the-job experience.

Not everyone strikes gold on his or her first direct contact or gets hired over the phone, but it is certainly possible. Realistically, prepare yourself to make as many as a dozen or more calls to get an interview and then to proceed with the normal interviewing process.

Again, in Chapter 8 you'll become thoroughly acquainted with job seeking and interviewing tactics that will grab you that position you've dreamed about.

Let's review what Scott did to make this fearless career change:

| | | |
|---|---|---|
| 1. Transferable talents | *Yes* | Had a bachelor's degree in art and a portfolio and some experience in building sets for theater. |
| 2. On-the-job training | *Yes* | The film industry always uses on-the-job training. |
| 3. Strategic education | No | |
| 4. Short-term education | No | |
| 5. Internship | No | |
| 6. Volunteering | No | |
| 7. Just Dive In! | *Yes* | A one-day career transition without any experience! |
| 8. Entrepreneurship | No | |

## From Attorney to Dog Trainer in 12 Weeks with Short-Term Education

**Name:** Han

**Former occupation:** Attorney

**New occupation:** Dog trainer

**Primary strategy:** Short-term training

**Other strategies:** Internship, entrepreneurship

**Length of time from career decision to a paid position:** 12 weeks
**Cost (if any) of transition:** $1,900

It can be difficult, coming from a society in which money and status are deemed to be two of the most important or the *only* important goals, to imagine that someone might want to give up both for a little peace of mind.

Yet, there are those who reach a point in their lives where no dollar amount on a paycheck can compensate for a feeling that their work has no meaning and no joy for them anymore.

That was exactly the case for Han. At the early age of 39, she had already been successful in a corporate law firm and was easily commanding a salary of over $350,000 a year. She also suffered from conditions that are sometimes attributed to stress. Chronic migraines and insomnia, coupled with recurrent depression, kept her from fully enjoying her ample earnings and a life full of opportunities.

Han said that her job was so consuming that she didn't even have time to date. She felt unhappy and isolated.

She had thought about getting out of law before, but she felt apprehensive because she really didn't have another plan of action. This year, she'd come to a breaking point. Somehow, she knew she had to get out of law and do something new. Han spent a long time trying to figure out what that was. When she performed the career fingerprinting process that you did at the beginning of the book, she came upon a unique talent that was, ironically, the very talent that attorneys use to win cases—persuasiveness.

Salespeople, teachers, and marketing and advertising executives use persuasiveness in their careers, but those careers didn't interest her. Neither did other forms of law like estate planning, criminal defense, divorce law, or entertainment law. In fact, nothing from the list of job titles you explored earlier in the book caught her fancy.

I asked her to make a list of the last five times she could remember being really happy. Her response went like this:

1. Watching the sunset over the ocean
2. Walking alone in a eucalyptus forest
3. Reading a great novel and drinking wine alone in the hot tub

4. "Dog sitting" for a friend
5. Stopping to pet a dog while jogging

"I think I like dogs better than people," she joked. "They're completely without guile, totally authentic. Dogs are better than the best antidepressant in the world." Odd that none of her happiest moments included people, and two out of five included dogs.

"What would you think about a career with animals?" She thought for a while. "Like what?" "Well, there are several," I replied. "Veterinarian, veterinary assistant, dog groomer, dog walker, opening a trendy doggie day spa or doggie day-care center, working with a volunteer group for the welfare of animals, being a dog trainer." As soon as I mentioned dog trainer, she became very animated. "That's something I'd like to look into," she said.

She researched the title on the O*NET. It was clear that Han was not going to make anywhere near $350,000 annually for being a dog trainer. In fact, the top ninetieth percentile of trainers in the United States made about $45,000 a year, according to this resource. Was she ready to take that kind of pay cut?

She was. Remembering how much she adored her childhood fox terrier and recalling how she was always the first to offer to babysit others' pets, she realized that the love she extended to animals and received in return was worth thousands, even tens of thousands, more than the emptiness and blandness of her experience of practicing law.

Han said something to me that I often hear when people find their authentic calling. "I would not only be a dog trainer for free, I'd even pay someone else just to be allowed to do it!" The feeling of *inner wealth* when doing the work that you love is often more than enough to trade for a high-paying job that doesn't strike a chord with who you really are. Han trained at a 12-week program that cost $1,900 dollars. From day 1 she reported feeling "happier than I can remember." Later, she did an informal, unpaid internship with a more experienced trainer. They led canine obedience classes together. Though Han was not paid, she was free to accept business from any of the dog owner students in the class who wanted private training.

This was one of the fundamental ways that she built her private business in animal obedience. I'll point out other techniques that Han used to become a successful entrepreneur in Chapter 8. A year later, Han tells me she's never regretted making the change and that she's finally found something "natural and effortless" to her.

Let's review the strategies that made Han's new career possible:

| | | |
|---|---|---|
| 1. Transferable talents | *Yes* | Persuasiveness. |
| 2. On-the-job training | No | |
| 3. Strategic education | No | |
| 4. Short-term education | *Yes* | A 12-week dog-training course. |
| 5. Internship | *Yes* | Cotaught canine obedience classes. |
| 6. Volunteering | No | |
| 7. Just Dive In! | *Yes* | She built her own clientele. |
| 8. Entrepreneurship | No | |

## A Promotion from Job Developer to Vocational Rehabilitation Counselor in Three Weeks Using Strategic Education

**Name:** Rodrigo

**Former occupation:** Job developer

**New occupation:** Vocational rehabilitation counselor

**Primary strategy:** Strategic education

**Other strategies:** Transferable talents, on-the-job training

**Length of time from career decision to a paid position:** Three weeks

**Cost (if any) of transition:** $450.00

Rodrigo was first hired in the early 1990s by a vocational rehabilitation firm that helped workers who were injured on the job to change or modify their occupations and get back to work. He was brought onboard as a *job developer*, someone who assists clients in learning the job search skills—such as resume writing and interviewing—to obtain employment. In some cases, the job developer makes contact with employers to get interviews for the client and/or to discuss how a client might engage in paid on-the-job training in an unfamiliar field.

Rodrigo wanted to take a step up to being a vocational rehabilitation counselor. Being a rehabilitation counselor would allow him to have more impact and influence on his clients' career decision-making process. He would be interfacing with the workers' doctors, lawyers, and training programs as well as being instrumental in helping them make choices about new career directions that would not aggravate their injuries.

Rodrigo knew that a master's degree in counseling or a related subject was necessary to move from a job developer to a full-fledged counselor. What he did not know was that the master's degree was a *preference,* not a *requirement.*

In other words, though a graduate degree was the industry standard, there was nothing ethically or legally stating that a person without that degree could not do the job.

---

*It is very important that when you read the job requirements for a certain career or position, that you understand the difference between preferred and required. A preferred requirement is usually one that may be overlooked if you have other attributes that interest the employer. A required qualification is something that is "hard and fast" because it is mandated by law. For example, a physician cannot practice medicine without first obtaining a medical degree and a license to practice, no matter what his or her intelligence or talents.*

---

Of course, there are some fields wherein advanced degrees are required, especially in the medical field, law, and academia. But many, if not most, degree requirements in other fields may be waived in favor of a person's possessing a superior background, speaking more than one language, or having specialized knowledge and other factors.

---

*If you have a BA and you see a job in the newspaper that asks for an MA, consider that requirement as part of a wish list.*

---

Research the position carefully to see if a certain degree or certification is mandated by law or simply expected by the employer. There is a vast difference between the two, and if you're not aware of it, you may miss a good opportunity to get hired in a position for which you are *qualified by experience* and for which an advanced degree is merely a preference.

Even if you are competing with others who might have superior academic qualifications, it is your *ability to communicate* how well you can help the employer *make a profit* that will win over any academic degree.

In Chapter 8, we'll talk about ways to present yourself, using what I call *Q statements*, which will enable you to *prove to the employer* that you will make the competitive difference—not by having a degree, but by having the ability to draw on past successes, to demonstrate, without a doubt, that you can bring more to the company than others competing for the same position.

---

**If you have enough of a certain kind of experience, or if, like Rodrigo, you are simply enrolled in a more advanced degree program, you may very well get the job despite not yet having the degree.**

---

When Rodrigo became aware of this fact, he discussed his plan with his employer. The employer agreed to promote him if he were to enroll in an MEd program (master's in educational counseling) at a local university. Not only that, the employer agreed to pay a tuition reimbursement of 50 percent. About a month into his classes, Rodrigo was promoted, and he received a substantial raise. Rodrigo was yet another person for whom strategic education really paid off. Rodrigo's $450 investment in strategic education resulted immediately in a 56 percent raise.

As a result of showing his employer *where he was headed,* he ended up getting a promotion that he would not have been eligible for had he not enrolled in a master's program.

Here is a picture of how Rodrigo gained the leverage for his promotion:

| 1. Transferable talents | *Yes* | Communication and working with clients. |
|---|---|---|
| 2. On-the-job training | *Yes* | Needed to acquire some new skills. |
| 3. Strategic education | *Yes* | Enrolled in a graduate course. |
| 4. Short-term education | No | |
| 5. Internship | No | |
| 6. Volunteering | No | |
| 7. Just Dive In! | No | |
| 8. Entrepreneurship | No | |

## From Administrative Assistant to Midwife Assistant in Four Weeks Using an Internship

**Name:** Caroline

**Former occupation:** Administrative assistant

**New occupation:** Midwife assistant

**Primary strategy:** Internship

**Other strategies:** On-the-job training, short-term education

**Length of time from career decision to a paid position:** Four weeks

**Cost (if any) of transition:** $300

Caroline told me that being laid off from her job as an administrative assistant was exactly the "wake-up call" she needed to let go of a position that she said she could "almost do in my sleep." Sometimes a layoff can bring a welcome relief if you didn't like your job anyway, especially when it is accompanied by a sizable severance package.

When she came in for career counseling, Caroline completed a career fingerprinting process in which she discovered that her principle and most cherished talent was "to nurture." She told me that, for years, she had wanted to be a midwife assistant, but like so many of us, she was so absorbed in "paying the bills" that she had little time to really think about how her authentic calling could come about.

*Midwife assistants* (also known as *doulas* or *labor assistants*) help fully certified midwives or doctors in prenatal, birthing, and postnatal care in either home, birth center, or hospital births.

Caroline knew what she wanted to do, and she decided to perform some research on just how to do it. She found out through her *labor market readiness research* that most birth centers and midwives (who were the most likely people to employ her) preferred a midwife certification program of study followed by an internship period with a reputable organization or licensed nurse midwife.

Four out of 10 potential workplaces mentioned a school in Seattle, Washington, that had a good reputation for turning out competent and employable midwives. Caroline put her severance package to use to pay for the cost of training and the waiting period (if any) she might need before her new career began. Her research revealed that training programs required from three weekends to three months of classes and attendance, as an internship at anywhere from 3 to 15 births. Schools cost from $300 to $4,500.

Caroline chose a school in Seattle that cost $425 for a three-day weekend set of seminars. Based on her research, she chose the school that fit her time and budget as well as having an *excellent placement rate* and a good name with employers. Within three months of study in school and observation of 11 births, Caroline was up and running—a new and fulfilling career awaiting her!

Here's another look at Caroline's strategies:

| | | |
|---|---|---|
| 1. Transferable talents | *Yes* | Interpersonal communication, nurturing. |
| 2. On-the-job training | *Yes* | Needed to acquire some new skills. |
| 3. Strategic education | No | |
| 4. Short-term education | *Yes* | Completed a three-day seminar. |
| 5. Internship | *Yes* | Observed and assisted in 11 live births. |
| 6. Volunteering | No | |
| 7. Just Dive In! | No | |
| 8. Entrepreneurship | No | |

## From Vice President of Human Resources to Career Coach in Six Weeks Using Transferable Talents

**Name:** Tom

**Former occupation:** Vice president, human resources

**New occupation:** Outplacement consultant and career coach

**Primary strategy:** Transferable talents

**Other strategies:** Entrepreneurship, short-term education

**Length of time from career decision to a paid position:** Six weeks

**Cost (if any) of transition:** $0.00

At age 55, Tom thought he would be ready for an early retirement in a few years. In the fall of that year, though, there were talks of a merger in the multinational telecommunications company where Tom had worked for 17 years. He was afraid, despite his seniority as a vice president of human resources, that his job might be impacted if indeed the merger were to take place.

While still working, Tom took some time to do his homework and went to several interviews with other telecommunications corporations as a backup plan. Tom confided in me later that, despite his youthful enthusiasm, vast experience, and excellent health, he was convinced that no job offers were materializing *simply because of his age.*

It is disheartening to think that there would be traces of ageism, especially in the otherwise progressive high-tech industry, but many of my clients have reported similar observations to me, and it seems apparent that many people who are over 50 have a similarly unfair experience.

---

*It can be frightening to even think about changing occupations in a job market that devalues your talents and experience because of an age bias, and this fear was something Tom had to face in his transition. Fortunately, it didn't stop him in his tracks. If this is a concern you have, don't let it stop you.*

---

As it turns out, Tom's position *was* eliminated as the result of the merger several months later, and he found himself without an office, a title, or a paycheck. Tom had hoped to work at least a few years longer. This was too early, even for an early retirement.

Fortunately, he left with an excellent severance package (a severance package may include cash, extended benefits, or other perks) and the use of free outplacement services to help him find a new position. Outplacement companies employ career counselors who assist entry-level to executive employees in managing their careers, particularly after a downsizing. The company that carried out the layoff pays their fees, and there is no charge for the downsized employees who attend.

Tom decided to take full advantage of the outplacement services, which included workshops, seminars, and individual career coaching. At some point, Tom's coach posed the possibility that with Tom's background and transferable talents from human resources, he might be an excellent candidate for becoming an outplacement consultant himself.

Tom jumped on the idea because he liked the possibility of the freedom the position promised. He could work on call for an outplacement company teaching seminars and coaching other executives and build a business on the side as a career coach (very similar to an outplacement consultant) in an independent private practice. He was free at any time to turn down work with the outplacement company without negative consequences. He would have some control over his flow of private clients, and he could therefore take off for a vacation whenever he wished. He could have the best of retirement—freedom and leisure—and the best of the working world—a high hourly fee, stimulating colleagues, and a prestigious title with a good company.

He found that, unlike his other unpleasant experiences in interviewing, the outplacement industry actually seemed to value his know-how and maturity. He interviewed with three companies in Atlanta, Georgia, and he received two offers. He accepted the offer with the highest pay scale. The company had a short and straightforward paid training program that lasted only two days.

He then did a very short four-day internship wherein he observed other coaches teaching seminars, while he got some practice teaching in front of a live audience. He was then certified as a consultant for that company. He started work the next week. Tom has become an entrepreneur (self-employed) with what is sometimes known as a *portfolio career* (a career having several avenues of income). He is an independent contractor for the outplacement company, he earns income from his private career coaching practice, and he is sometimes paid to lead seminars for church, school, and professional organizations.

If you are planning on becoming a successful consultant like Tom, I suggest that you read *The Consultant's Guide to Publicity* by Reece Franklin.* It will show you how to become well known in your field with a minimum monetary investment.

> *If you want to "brand" yourself as a consultant with a national or worldwide reputation in your field, there is no better way than to write a book and/or get quoted as an expert in major newspapers and magazines.*

Also, Dan Janal, who has a Web site at www.prleads.com, is a fantastic resource to get you started on getting quoted by the best newspapers and creating the *expert image* that is so important if you are to attract business and be a leader in your profession.

Here's a review of Tom's fearless career change strategies:

| | | |
|---|---|---|
| 1. Transferable talents | *Yes* | HR concerns itself with matters of jobs and employment |
| 2. On-the-job training | No | |
| 3. Strategic education | No | |
| 4. Short-term education | *Yes* | He took a paid two-day in-house seminar. |
| 5. Internship | *Yes* | He did a paid four-day internship. |
| 6. Volunteering | No | |

*Reece Franklin, *The Consultants's Guide to Publicity, How to Make a Name for Yourself by Promoting Your Expertise*, Wiley, New York, 1996.

| | | |
|---|---|---|
| 7. Just Dive In! | No | |
| 8. Entrepreneurship | *Yes* | He opened his own career coaching private practice. |

## From Corporate Events Planner to CEO in 12 Weeks Using Entrepreneurship

**Name:** Alice

**Former occupation:** Events planner

**New occupation:** CEO, discount travel and entertainment company

**Primary strategy:** Entreprenership

**Other strategies:** Just Dive In!, transferable talents

**Length of time from career decision to a paid position:** Three months

**Cost (if any) of transition:** U.S. Small Business Administration and home-equity loans (explained below)

It would be hard for most of us to imagine a job that was more fun than Alice's. Alice had the good fortune of being an events planner for a well-known computer company in Texas. She scheduled corporate events like large-scale seminars, picnics, and fairs. In addition to planning internal events, she was in charge of booking travel, entertainment, and sporting events for executives and employees of the company.

Because her company was so large and so many people were interested in these events, Alice was sometimes able to negotiate discounts of up to 60 percent from vendors for theater, opera, sports, cruises, and a host of other goods and services. For most of us, this might have been a job to keep for life, but Alice had a special dream of starting her own discount travel and entertainment business where customers could buy tickets on the Internet, and she had a strong calling to be a philanthropist.

Right at the heart of Alice's plan was the idea that for every ticket sold, 30 percent of the profits would go to charities and nonprofit organizations. It was *absolutely essential* to Alice that she oversaw a company that was committed to giving back to the community. Her talent, as she saw it, was philanthropy. Owning her own company was only a vehicle for her to be able to give generously to her community.

Like many of the people we've talked about in this book, Alice's wake-up call came when her employer was downsizing due to its shifting of much of its computer manufacturing to factories outside the United States.

Alice sought advice about how to get her business up and running. She was referred to the Small Business Administration (www.sba.gov), a department of the U.S. government with offices in most cities.

---

**The SBA assists entrepreneurs in starting and improving their businesses. They give free classes in starting a business, getting government and private loans for businesses, small-business bookkeeping and accounting, sales and marketing, and other topics of interest to people starting new companies.**

---

Alice would be able to consult, for free, with a mentor (someone who had already started a successful business) through a government-funded program called SCORE (www.score.org). Establishing a working relationship with one or more of the expert counselors from SCORE is one of the first steps you should take if you wish to start an enduringly successful business. You might pay up to $500 an hour for this kind of consulting elsewhere, but at SCORE it will cost you nothing!

By attending classes at the SBA and working with her mentor from SCORE, Alice found the best way to fund her new business. She was somewhat concerned because her credit score was far from perfect, but she was able to receive a $15,000 microloan cosponsored by the Small Business Administration and a private bank.

It took only 10 days from the day she filled out a simple form to the day her bank account was credited with the funding. In addition, because she owned a home, she was also able to borrow $70,000 against her equity in the home by refinancing her original mortgage.

Like almost every small-business owner, Alice wore many hats at the beginning of her enterprise: Web designer, owner, administrative assistant, bookkeeper, marketing director—and, well, you get the picture. Later she was able to assemble an executive staff and pay them a monthly stipend until the business was off and running.

Eventually, she hired a Web designer, a chief technical officer, a chief marketing officer, an executive vice president, and a chief financial officer. Alice is in the final phases of completing her Web site, but she already has a full house for several events—to Broadway plays, a trip to Las Vegas, and a 12-day Mediterranean cruise.

For all her hard work, Alice and three of her family members are traveling for free, but what satisfies her most is that *30 percent of the profits* from all these events will be going to adult literacy, AIDS prevention, and breast cancer research.

Alice's success can be attributed to the following strategies:

| | | | |
|---|---|---|---|
| 1. Transferable talents | *Yes* | Developed same skills as an employee. | |
| 2. On-the-job training | *Yes* | She had to learn how to run her own business. | |
| 3. Strategic education | No | | |
| 4. Short-term education | *Yes* | Free SBA classes. | |
| 5. Internship | No | | |
| 6. Volunteering | No | | |
| 7. Just Dive In! | *Yes* | From employee to CEO! | |
| 8. Entrepreneurship | *Yes* | She started her business from "scratch." | |

## From Retirement to Jewelry Designer in Eight Weeks Using Transferable Talents

**Name:** Elsie

**Former occupation:** Retired

**New occupation:** Jewelry and crafts designer

**Primary strategy:** Transferable skills

**Other strategies:** Just Dive In!, entrepreneurship

**Length of time from career decision to a paid position:** Two months

**Cost (if any) of transition:** Up-front costs for materials

Elsie, at age 72, had been enjoying retirement on her late husband's military pension for over 10 years. She was busy, healthy, and content for most of those years until her son, granddaughters, and daughter-in-law moved out of state. Without the support and warmth of her family, she suddenly experienced a void.

She came to career counseling saying that she wanted to return to part-time work but she wasn't sure she had the skills. In her active working years when Elsie was a secretary for a large insurance firm, she used a typewriter—not a computer—and she feared that going back to work as a secretary would mean learning to use computers. It was not an area into which she wanted to venture, and I could tell from her voice and body language that being a secretary was no longer of interest to her. She certainly wasn't desperate for money, and she wanted to do something meaningful and fun.

What we uncovered with the career fingerprinting process was that Elsie was an artist. For years she had been doing oil painting, making wooden toys for children, and designing and making jewelry in her spare time, but she *never thought she could make money at it.*

When she examined her fears about stepping out into the marketplace after so many years of retirement, she figured she had nothing to lose. She decided to give it a try. First, she began displaying her custom-made jewelry at local street fairs and charitable events. She was happily surprised that people were actually willing to pay up to $300 for her beautifully designed necklaces and bracelets.

After building her confidence for a few months by witnessing other people's excitement about her work, she began to approach retail stores and sell her items to them in bulk. Soon, she had more orders than she could handle and had to hire an apprentice.

Elsie, once unable to even balance her checkbook, was now taking Visa and MasterCard. She never, to my knowledge, learned how to handle a computer, but that was okay—her assistant did that for her. Elsie is as active as ever, and her jewelry seems to be giving joy to many people.

---

**Often, we find our true calling is a hobby like photography, planning weddings, fixing cars, doing historical research, electronics troubleshooting, cooking, sewing, writing, drama, or sports.**

---

Elsie is a great example of someone who took the transferable talents from her hobby and turned them into a profit-making enterprise.

Here's a brief capsule of how Elsie used her resources to make a fearless career change:

| | | |
|---|---|---|
| 1. Transferable talents | *Yes* | She transformed her hobby into a business. |
| 2. On-the-job training | No | |
| 3. Strategic education | No | |
| 4. Short-term education | No | |
| 5. Internship | No | |
| 6. Volunteering | *Yes* | At first, auctioned some work at charity events. |
| 7. Just Dive In! | *Yes* | With no extra training, she just took the plunge! |
| 8. Entrepreneurship | *Yes* | She started and ran her own business. |

## Key Strategies

You've just taken in a lot of information, so stop for a moment and think about the strategies you like—the ones that seem to best suit your own personality. Also, take some time to determine which of these strategies (or perhaps other strategies of your own) you'd like to use in your next career change.

Strategies I like:

1. _____

2. _____

3. _____

4. _____

5. _____

Other:

_____

_____

_____

_____

_____.

Most practical strategies for my next career change:

1. _____

2. _____

3. _____

4. _____

5. _____

Other:

_____

_____

_____

_____

_____.

In the next chapter, on goal setting, you'll use the strategies you've selected to devise a plan of action. Then you'll move on to the next phase—enacting your plan with accelerated job search techniques.

# CHAPTER SEVEN

# Setting and Reaching Enticing Goals

How to set goals is one of the most important things you can learn in your life. It is a skill that can guide and transform every area of life from your health and finances to your social, spiritual, physical, and career pursuits.

> **Once you learn the goal-setting techniques in this chapter, you'll find that setting goals is a simple and straightforward process.**

As you begin to reap the rewards from regularly writing your objectives and making realistic plans to meet them, you may choose to make goal setting a lifelong tool.

## Studies on Goal Setting

The two anecdotes I'm about to tell you are almost folklore in the fields of self improvement and human motivation, but just in case you've never read them in a book before or heard them at a seminar,

I want to make sure you get these stories under your belt and really put the lessons in them to use.

The first story involves the graduating class of an Ivy League university in the 1950s. The researchers asked every member of the class, "Do you have clear, measurable goals?" As the story goes, only 10 percent of the class reported that they had clear, measurable goals.

This study was a *longitudinal study*, meaning that the behavior, attitudes, or conditions of a group or individual were examined first at one time and then again at a much later time. In the case of this first study, the graduating class was looked at first in one decade and again (that is, those who could be found and were still alive) in two more decades.

When the researchers contacted the surviving members of the class 20 years later, they found that the *10 percent of the class* who had stated that they had clear, measurable goals had, on average, an income *seven times higher* than that of the former students who did not report having goals.

Shortly afterward, another group of researchers from another prominent university saw this evidence published. The researchers wanted to try the same experiment with a bit of a "spin" on it. This time they took the graduating class of their own university and asked the question, "Which of you have clear, measurable, *written* goals?" *Only 3 percent* this time reported that they not only had clear, measurable goals but they also had committed their goals to writing.

When the surviving members of this second group of subjects were examined 20 years later, it was found that the minute 3 percent of men and woman who had clear, measurable *written* goals were worth, financially speaking, *10 times more* than the *entire* remaining 97 percent of the class combined.

You may or may not believe in the power of setting goals, but the studies recounted above strongly suggest that knowing how to set goals and, especially, writing them down are skills that are closely related to our performance and achievement.

> *Almost all truly great achievers have some sort of system of conceptualizing their future goals and using methods to bring their desired objectives about.*

Some may use a more formal system like the one you will learn. Others may think of their goals as mere "daydreams" and write them down, less formally, in a journal. Some people find it relaxing to make drawings and/or flowcharts of their intentions in a notebook.

I have known people who jot down all their goals on a piece of paper and place that paper in a special box or a special file and then review their progress once a month. Others only think clearly and intently about their goals or, perhaps, share their aims with just one trusted person, and, even though their goals are not written, their intensity of purpose and commitment to action brings about the result they planned on.

## Setting Balanced Goals

To be sure, truly successful people conceive of goals for every part of their lives—not just career goals. This holistic approach to goal setting reminds you that happiness and success are the fruits of a balanced life that includes social, spiritual, recreational, financial, fitness, health, and other elements of existence.

Although there are many areas for which to fashion new and exciting goals, we're going to begin with focusing on your career goal since I assume you're reading this book because you're interested in making a quick and economical career change. However, once you learn to design and actualize your career goals, you will be able to use the same formula to achieve goals in other areas of your life.

## Steps for Writing an Attainable Goal

### Step 1. Write a Clear, Measurable Statement of Your Goal, Described in the Present Tense, Using an Exact Calendar Date for Its Attainment

An example of this sort of goal statement is, "I now have a wonderful career as a certified financial planner on June 17, 20xx."

Why do we write the goal in the present tense? Because if you say "I will" rather than "I am" your brain will subconsciously keep putting that goal off into the future.

It may also seem odd to write an exact calendar date for a goal whose attainment on a specific day cannot be precisely predicted.

In spite of the seemingly impossible task of predicting an exact date, the majority of people I have worked with who use this method actually end up attaining their goals within a week or two of the stated calendar date.

Again, your subconscious mind has a better chance of *keeping you on track* if you provide it with a *specific guideline* as to when the goal will be realized.

## Step 2. Design Your Goal So That It's Both Believable and Attainable

It's one thing to think big and imagine great things for yourself. It's another to plan for something that is so outrageously unattainable that even you have a hard time believing it could really happen.

For example, it may not be at all unreasonable to write a goal saying "I now make $7,000 a month as a presales hardware engineer on September 9, 2006," but it is rather doubtful that you could make, let's say, a million dollars a month in that position.

Though I encourage you to dream, it's best when goal setting to commit to goals that are humanly attainable. Then when you reach your goal of making $7,000 a month, you can always set another goal for an incremental increase of your income.

## Step 3. You Must Have a Workable Plan to Reach Your Goal

Your new career will probably not come about by sheer magic. It's important to consider the concrete steps you need to take to make your dream happen. Those steps may include raising or saving a certain amount of money and/or applying one or more of the fearless career change strategies discussed in detail in Chapters 8 and 9, such as working in an internship position or enrolling in a short-term education program, or taking the steps needed to implement your job search or to start your new business.

It is also important to note any obstacles *(inside or outside of you)* that might prevent you from reaching your goal. For almost everyone navigating a major career transition, fear is likely to rear its head. You're no different from most people if you feel some trepidation on the road to your dreams.

This takes us back to the very beginning of this book when you wrote down the fears that you associate with change. It may be that when setting your goal, you'll notice a bit of anxiety well up again. Refer back to the first chapter and review your record of dealing with fear and risks successfully in the past, and remember that if you did it then, you can also master your fear now.

Perhaps your obstacle is an external rather than an internal block. Maybe, for example, you are a single parent and your young child needs babysitting at night while you go to the evening seminars you need in order to make your move into your new vocation. Perhaps you don't have enough money to afford both the seminars and child care. This brings us to the last step in the goal-setting formula.

## Step 4. Brainstorm Ways to Break Through or Get Around the Obstacles to Your Goal

*Brainstorming* means allotting a short time, perhaps 2 to 10 minutes to write down every single thing you can think of that would solve the problem, no matter how remote or silly it might sound. Inviting friends or family for a group brainstorming session can also be quite effective.

In brainstorming by yourself or with others, you may come up with solutions like "trading" child care with a neighbor who also has children, winning the lottery, taking on an extra job, standing on the street with a sign saying "put me through school," or getting a loan to help defray your costs.

Of course, some of those solutions are ridiculous, but brainstorming helps your mind be more creative and uninhibited. Out of all the solutions you write, it's likely that one or two will be feasible.

You could ask the neighbors to watch your child for the time it takes to complete the seminars, and you can return the favor and watch their children at a later date. Or you can get on the phone to your mom in St. Louis and see if she wouldn't mind staying in the guest room for a few weeks and watching her "little angel." (You know she won't mind!)

If you simply cringe at the thought of living with Mom cleaning up after you and giving unsolicited advice, you might consider trimming one of your preferred activities or products as we did earlier in your "transition budget"—even if it means putting off buying that wide-screen TV for now or cutting back on the cell phone minutes so you can afford a sitter.

Whatever your obstacle, brainstorming—that is, writing down every single possibility you can think of within a given time limit—will almost surely present you with one or more workable alternatives to chip away at those barriers.

Let's look at the goal statement on the next page, which is one Miguel wrote preceding his new job as a financial planner.

## Your Own Goal Worksheet

For this exercise, take the career that you determined earlier and elaborate on it in goal-oriented language. Fill out the goal template on page 124 with your own data, using the information in Miguel's goal worksheet as a guide. For now, if you aren't sure about a date or about the cost of something, do some research, if possible, and then write your best guess.

Your telephone is your most valuable tool in guessing about the price of something. Call a few stores or schools to get the prices for the things or classes you need. Take the price of three of the same things, add them up, and divide by three. That way you can at least anticipate the average amount of an item or educational program you'll need. You can always adjust the amount at a later time to be more accurate.

Great! Remember, you can use the work you've just done on your career goal for many of the other goals you set for yourself. I don't expect you to construct goals for every area of your life right now (unless you really want to). First, I recommend that you get some practice at focusing on and working toward one goal at a time. Later, you'll be more adept at the process and will be able to juggle multiple goals simultaneously. For now:

- Read your *career goal* once each morning and once each night.
- Begin taking the steps needed to reach your goal and implementing solutions to any perceived obstacles. *Check your progress at least once a week.* Are you following through on your plan of action? What measurable progress (like phone calls, purchases, sending letters, reading, research) have you made?
- *Mentally rehearse* your goal once or twice a day. (More on this idea later.)

**Goal statement:** "I now have a position as a financial advisor with Henley, Scott, and Thompson making $65,000 per year on October 22, 20xx."

**Date:** October 22, 20xx

**Materials or things needed and cost**
New briefcase, $90
Financial calculator, $60
Two new suits, $600
Four new ties, $80
Palm Pilot, $350

**People and organizations to contact and cost**
E-mail news of career change to friends, family, former associates (this will be a good source of referrals when building my client base), $0
International Association of Electrical Engineers (IEEE). Attending luncheons and other functions will also attract clients from my old profession. Consider possibility of being a speaker. Annual membership fee, $160

**Knowledge and/or education needed and cost**
Must pass 12-week basic training, $0
Must take and pass Series 63 Licensing Exam, exam fee, $220
Must take and pass Series 7 Licensing Exam, exam fee, $80
Learn how to manage a Microsoft Outlook calendar, contact database, and task list to keep myself organized. Cost of CD tutorial, $40

**Potential obstacle(s)**
I don't feel like I have a "sales" type of personality.

**Ways to overcome the obstacle(s)**
Join Toastmasters to learn public speaking.
Go to the library and check out books on sales.
Role-play sales situations with people I know.

*Sample Goal Worksheet for Miguel*

**Goal statement:**

_____

_____

**Date:** _____

**Materials or things needed**    **Cost**

_____  _____

_____  _____

_____  _____

_____  _____

_____  _____

**People and organizations to contact**  **Cost**

_____  _____

_____  _____

_____  _____

_____  _____

_____  _____

**Knowledge and/or education needed**  **Cost**

_____  _____

_____  _____

_____  _____

_____  _____

_____  _____

**Potential obstacle(s)**

_____

_____

**Ways to overcome the obstacle(s)**

_____

_____

_____

*Your Sample Goal Worksheet*

Goals are the places where dreams and actions meet. Pick out the kinds of goals that *motivate you* and give you pleasure to think about, and then make them materialize with your *sustained and persistent efforts*. Success requires action!

# *Mental Rehearsal*

Extensive research in the fields of sports, psychology, peak performance, and medicine has proven that visualizing your goal (picturing it vividly in your imagination with your eyes closed) will help you get there that much faster and achieve it with a greater degree of precision. Sometimes visualization is called *mental rehearsal* because that's exactly what it is—a moving picture with sound, smell, temperature, faces, shapes, and actions all perceived from your own viewpoint. It is as if you are actually in the scene, a part of the picture, hearing the sounds, smelling the smells.

A visualization is something you design for yourself to help you "rehearse" the outcomes of your goals. For example, if you'd like to be very relaxed on your first day in your brand-new career, you might design a mental rehearsal session for yourself that placed you in your new office feeling very comfortable, at ease, and confident.

If you close your eyes, you can construct this office in an ideal way for yourself—see the furniture, windows, desk, and what's on your desk. You may notice that someone enters your office with a smile on her face, and all the while you are feeling very relaxed and confident. You might even imagine your boss saying "Good job!" at the end of the day or someone who looks interesting inviting you out for lunch.

You can create anything you wish in your ideal rehearsal, and the more detailed you are—the more you see vibrant colors, hear the qualities of people's voices talking, really imagine how you feel as you talk to a client or customer, and even sense the temperature of the room you're in—the more you are likely to feel the emotions you'd like to feel when the real day arrives.

Professional athletes have been using this technique for decades to make field goals, score baskets, win contests, and break records. Consider it for yourself, and have some fun with it!

If you don't want to make up your own rehearsal, you might buy an audiocassette tape or CD with a prerecorded generic mental rehearsal on it. Most of these recordings help you picture yourself in any situation you like and handling it at your very best, usually in a very relaxed, comfortable, competent way.

An excellent author of these recordings is Dr. Emmett Miller, a physician who has worked for over 20 years with top athletes and entertainers. He is considered to be at the forefront of the science of mental rehearsal. His audio recordings are available for purchase on his Web site (www.drmiller.com), and they are highly recommended.

Merely acting on impulse or putting one foot in front of the other without a clear compass delineating where you're headed will simply leave you in lost dreams and frustrations. That's why it's important to take the steps described in this chapter.

Goal setting is a serious business, but you may find yourself having fun as you realize that you really do have the power to bring your fantasies to fruition. I know you can set concrete goals and make plans to meet them. In Chapter 8 we're going to put those goals into purposeful action.

# CHAPTER EIGHT

# The Accelerated Job Search

Now that you've identified your destination and you've planned a way to get there, the next step is to take action. In this chapter you'll learn how to apply the strategies for accelerated job searching. You'll also receive examples of résumés, cover letters, and special phone scripts to use as tools to help you land your dream job.

## The Accelerated Job Search Process

Making your journey to the job you really want in the fastest way possible is the aim of this chapter, and there are six important skills to learn in the process:

1. Stacking the odds of getting an interview in your favor
2. Writing your own fearless career change résumé
3. Writing approach, cover, confirmation, and other relevant letters
4. Using direct-contact techniques to secure job interviews
5. Applying fearless career change interviewing techniques
6. Discerning when and how to follow up on phone calls, letters, and interviews

# How to Beat the Competition by Interrupting the Hiring Cycle

In a common hiring cycle, a new job opening appears when *someone who has the power to hire you* perceives that there is a need for a new person in a project, department, office, or organization.

This idea to hire may have arisen for a number of reasons: someone quit, someone was fired, someone died or moved out of the area, or someone is out because of an extended period of illness and it's not clear if that person is going to return.

It also could mean that a higher head count is needed in the company because there is a new product or service that needs fresh ideas or because an executive or manager needs a second person in charge. There are a score of other reasons.

## Four Phases of the Hiring Cycle

In the fearless career change methodology, we have a way of bypassing—even eliminating—the competition by *interrupting* what I call the *hiring cycle* before it reaches the final phase. It's important to understand each stage to know how to interrupt it at the advantageous moment.

*Phase 1.* While the hiring manager who sees the necessity of bringing on someone new first has the idea in his or her mind, only *one* person (namely, the person with the idea) knows that there is a possibility of a job opening. In most cases, this decision maker has to get permission from a *higher* decision maker.

*Phase 2.* While the decision maker and his or her superior are discussing the potential hire (which, in larger companies, can take up to a month or more), *only two or three* people know that there is a possibility of a job opening. If the senior person approves the hire, it will be submitted to the human resources department.

*Phase 3.* In the human resources department, a job description, in-house announcements, advertisements, a pay scale, and legal documents pertaining to the position are drawn up. This part of the process can take from three to nine months, depending on the size of the company. The opening may be announced internally, and up to 300 people may know of its existence. At this point, the competition is somewhat higher but not insurmountable.

*Phase 4.* The employment opening is announced to the general public via various media such as newspapers, the Internet, the radio, or trade journals. Experts estimate that at this phase your competition skyrockets to as many as 10,000 or more potential job applicants.

## The Unadvertised Job Market

Remember, *no one* in the general public has yet to hear of the new posting until it reaches phase 4 of the hiring cycle. Because phases 1 through 3 are "hidden" from the outside world, they are also sometimes referred to as the *hidden job market* or the *unadvertised job market.*

---

**The unadvertised job market is your window
of opportunity.**

---

If you were somehow to hear of a potential opening at phase 2 or 3, you would have *only a handful* of other people competing for the opening.

If you had a way to directly reach the decision maker in phase 1 *when it was first conceived,* you would not have *any* competition. That's it. *Zero!*

## Beating the Job Search Statistics

Let's take a look at what happens if you wait to see the opening in the classifieds of your local newspaper. As mentioned before, as many as *10,000 other people* may see that ad, take interest in it, and become your competition. The numbers go up astronomically when you think about the millions of people around the world who have access to a job opening when it's advertised on the Internet!

This is not to say that you should *never* open a newspaper again if you're looking for a job. Newspapers, networking, and the Internet are still viable means to get a job. Used along with direct-contact techniques aimed at the unadvertised job market, they are an important part of the job search. Just make sure that you don't spend too much of your valuable time focused on advertisements.

Now that you understand the difference between the advertised and the unadvertised job market, you can undoubtedly see why many career coaches are beginning to advocate the use of direct-contact techniques in the unadvertised job market. Finding an unadvertised job opening is somewhat of a numbers game. Studies show that anywhere from 1 in 12 direct-contact phone calls (in a healthy job market) will yield an opening and that the odds of finding an opportunity in a slower market are 1 in 20. Can you predict an opening in the unadvertised job market before placing a call or sending a letter of inquiry? It's difficult, but several guidelines can help you choose the kinds of companies that are more likely to present potential positions.

1. It's important to remember that very large companies in the process of massively downsizing may also be hiring at the same time. That's because layoffs usually take place by job function or departments rather than by arbitrary numbers. Hundreds, even thousands, can get laid off in the manufacturing department while scores of people are getting hired in sales or human resources. Similarly, sales could be waning while manufacturing is booming! A company may be skimming off upper-management positions while actively hiring for entry-level functions.

   Therefore, just because you read in the newspaper that there has been a huge layoff at a company does not mean that you should omit that company from your list of potential workplaces.

2. There is no way to make an absolute judgment about how many people might be hired at some point in the future, but there are ways to make educated guesses about the probability that an organization is increasing its head count. Two ways to make such a determination are with the help of the following resources:

   • Your local newspaper, the *Wall Street Journal, INC.* magazine, or *Forbes* magazine. Find stories that mention a local plant or corporation is opening new offices in your area. These offices and plants will need staffing and management even though the company may not be advertising the openings yet.

     The same thing applies to companies conspicuously reporting new projects or products. They may not need someone today, but when the project starts or the product is being manufactured and marketed, employees, managers, and sales teams will be needed to support those efforts.

- Use the Internet. One of my favorite sites for business information is www.hoovers.com. You can enter the name of several companies in the specialized Hoover's search engine and compare their one-year employee growth rates. At least relatively, you could determine lesser and better chances of openings arising in the near future. A 5.6 percent employee growth rate versus a rate of 21.7 percent can be found in two companies in the same industry that are practically next door to each other. Ironically, the company that seems more famous and successful may have a much lower growth rate than a lesser-known company.

    Hoover's also contains current news with clues about company expansion and implosion. You can find releases (things the company writes about itself, versus news, which is written by journalists and reporters). New-product releases and project initiations are often announced well ahead of the point that a company would normally hire people to staff these new ventures. Geographic data as well as companies' intentions to create new locations or new offices and factories are also reported in press releases. The classified ads in newspapers and on the Internet don't reflect these changes because they haven't happened yet. Again, if you uncover these clues, you'll be the first there with little or no competition for upcoming positions.

- Another useful site is vcbuzz.com. This site issues reports when start-up companies receive large infusions of venture capital (funding). Guess what happens after funding? You guessed it: hiring!

## Beginning Your Direct-Contact Campaign

Advertised or unadvertised, you are most likely going to need a résumé to make your career transition and job search successful. There are three basic types of résumés: *chronological, functional,* and *hybrid,* which is a combination of the first two.

When making a career change, you should probably use a chronological format, which is contrary to the traditional advice given to job searchers. I recommend chronological because in my experience, employers strongly prefer a chronological format. Please refer to the sample résumé later in this chapter for an example.

## How to Write Your Fearless Career Change Résumé

According to several surveys of hiring managers and human resources professionals in larger Fortune 500 companies, as many as *1,500 résumés* can pile up on one person's desk in as little time as a week.

> **These managers, department heads, and human resource professionals admit that they read only about the first five or six lines at the top of the résumé—about three to seven seconds' worth!**

That means that we *must* get the employer's attention within that crucial seven seconds of that first look. Here's how to do it.

### Streamline Your Objective

The first step in preparing your résumé to grab the reader in the first few seconds is to streamline your job objective (see sample résumé). Several years ago, it was popular to write objectives that sounded something like this:

> Seeking a challenging position that will leverage my interpersonal skills, business savvy, and technical know-how to make a significant contribution to the company, with the potential for continuous growth and advancement.

How long did it take you to read that sentence? About two or three seconds? Well, once that time is over, so is your first chance at "hooking" the employer's attention.

A fearless career change résumé uses *only a job title* to express the objective. That way, the employer knows *immediately* what you want and can get to the "meat" of the next few lines of your résumé right away. Here are examples of a fearless career change objective statement:

- A position as an environmental planner
- Environmental planner
- Biotechnical sales manager
- Licensed clinical social worker
- A position as a systems analyst

If you *must* write a more general objective, try to at least specify the *industry* and the *level* of position you're aiming for:

- An entry-level position in the sports management industry
- A managerial position in the food services field
- An executive position with a telecommunications start-up firm

If you're writing your résumé to a company that already has a written or advertised description of the job, try to use the exact same title on your résumé as the one in the written description.

## Compose a High-Impact Summary Statement

Your next tactic in swiftly capturing the reader's attention, while at the same time presenting almost all the information he or she needs to evaluate your readiness for an interview, is to pack the summary statement (which follows your objective) with an abundance of relevant, specific, and attention-getting information.

Your summary statement can be read in that *sensitive seven seconds*, and it provides the reader with a powerful first impression. Here are some sample summary statements to use as a guide:

> Over 10 years' experience as a landscaper and landscape
> designer as the owner of Big Bear Landscapes, specializing in
> native plants, low-maintenance gardens, and waterfall design.
> Responsible for landscaping a 12-acre property with low-main-
> tenance native plants, coming in eight days under deadline and
> $1,300 under budget. BS biology, Yale University. Currently
> enrolled in a course of study leading to a master's degree in
> environmental planning at California State University at
> Burlingame. Flexible, dependable, adaptable to change.

Over six years as an electrical engineer in a Fortune 500 company, specializing in wireless communications, project management, and testing. Won the Employee of the Year Award in 2000 and 2003. Master's in electrical engineering from the University of Georgia at Atlanta. Currently possess a series 65 and series 7 license and have passed a 12-week financial advisor training program at Henley, Scott, and Thomas, LLC. Trustworthy, proactive, detail oriented.

Over three years as a customer service representative for a nationally known health insurance carrier, specializing in customer satisfaction, troubleshooting, and training new employees. Handle over 200 customer inquiries daily, with only 3 percent escalation rate. Bachelor's degree in art from the University of California at Berkeley. Currently enrolled in courses leading to a certificate in video arts at the University of California, Santa Cruz. Reliable, creative, energetic.

Notice that these summary statements share a similar format. Each is three to five sentences long and no more. Every sentence has a very deliberate function. Let's take a look at what information each of them contains.

1. The first sentence states the number of years' experience in a given job title and industry and three areas of specialization. If you do your research on the O*NET, labor market readiness research, or by other means, you'll discover what "specializations" certain industries or employers demand. Since your résumé can and should change with every company to accommodate that company's preferences, your specializations can also change. For example, a human resources professional's résumé might say, "specializing in staffing, team building, and triaging" for one employer, but the wording might be altered for another organization to read "specializing in benefits, compensation, and sexual harassment issues." Same basic résumé—different companies, hence different specializations.

2. In the second sentence, pick out an accomplishment that will really dazzle the employer. Just because this accomplishment may have been achieved in a school, training, volunteer, hobby, or an intern situation does not mean that it's not relevant. Treat your achievement just as you would if you

had accomplished it at a paying job. For example, a computer networking professional just out of a certification class can still say, "Handled networking protocols for TCP/IP and wireless function on Linux and Solaris platforms." If you can, make your accomplishment into a Q statement (that is, an assertion that is quantified) like, "Built seven custom homes within a nine month period managing a crew of 12 construction workers."

3. Introduce your past educational background, if it applies to the job you're seeking, in the third sentence, and in the fourth, note your short-term education, strategic education, or other strategies. A great way to describe a training program that's not yet finished or just getting underway is "currently enrolled in a course of study leading to . . ." or "currently completing a degree in _____."

4. Last, you can list some of the personal strengths (not skills) that you bring to the table. Personal strengths are things like dependability, flexibility, and the ability to work well under pressure.

After reviewing the summary statements, write one for yourself using the following summary statement template. *Fill in the blanks on the template and leave out the italicized words.*

After you finish your statement, ask yourself (or maybe someone else!) these questions:

- Does my summary statement read like a "mini-résumé"?
- Does the summary grab the reader's attention and make a powerful impact?

## Turn Your Accomplishments into Q Statements

Q statements (an abbreviation for *quantified statements*) use quantifiable terms—numbers, percentages, amounts of time or things, and, occasionally, rating scales—to present your accomplishments in concrete, measureable ways. Here are some examples of Q statements:

- Decreased waste by 20 percent, resulting in an overall savings of $1.2 million a year.

Over ____ years as a _____ in the
_____industry, specializing in
_____, _____, and
_____. *[See below for how
to write a Q statement and write one that most pertains to the
type of skills you'll be using in your next job.]*

_____

_____

_____

BA *(or AA, BS, MBA, PhD, etc.)* in _____
from the University of _____. Currently
enrolled in a course of study leading to a _____
in _____ at _____ College.
*[Write three personal traits that describe you and most closely match
qualities you'll need on your next job—for example, dependable, team
player, learns quickly* _____, _____,
_____.

*Résumé Summary Statement Template*

- Attained gross annual sales of $193,000.
- Operated a multiline phone system and personally handled over 200 calls per day.
- Acted as a regional manager for 12 offices overseeing 147 salespeople throughout the Midwest.
- Initiated and developed a retraining program that improved employee satisfaction from 2.7 to 4.1 on a scale of 1 to 5.
- Decreased production time by six days a month, resulting in a savings of $360,000 quarterly.
- Maintained a caseload of 65 patients.
- Built a prototype that could tolerate 15 percent more stress than its predecessor.

- Introduced an on-site safety program that decreased workers' compensation claims by 18 percent in one year.
- Processed more than 250 customer requests daily.
- Won an award for decreasing materials costs from $6.41 per inch to $5.20 per inch.
- Instrumental in increasing customer satisfaction (on a scale of 1 to 10) from 3.0 to 7.5.

Once you start thinking of your job responsibilities as *measurable* accomplishments, Q statements will come easily to you and you can incorporate them into your résumé. It's not always possible to use a Q statement to describe what you did, but, no matter how small the accomplishment, there is usually a way to find a quantifiable value to include on your résumé. Take a look at how Q statements are incorporated into the sample résumé. Take a few moments now to write a first draft of your résumé using the sample résumé as your guide.

This résumé checklist will ensure that your résumé is sharp, powerful, and influential to the reader:

- ❑ The objective is crisp and concise. Just a job title if possible.
- ❑ Your summary presents a powerful picture, in just a few seconds, of what you can do.
- ❑ The bulleted statements are *quantified* wherever possible.
- ❑ The *years only* (and not the months) of employment are included.
- ❑ If you had more than one title at the same company, you place the *cumulative* years you were at the company at the top on the same line as the name of the company and the years you were in each *different* position next to the name of the job title in parentheses. (See sample résumé, "Anderson's Nursery").
- ❑ Going back into the job history more than 10 years is avoided. (This is true except in cases wherein a job more than 10 years ago has information that directly pertains to the job for which you're now applying.)
- ❑ Dates of college graduation are omitted. (In case the employer makes a judgment that you are too young or too old for the position.)

❑ It is all right to repeat items from your summary in the body of the résumé.

❑ There are no more than six and no fewer than two bullets under each job heading.

❑ You never refer to yourself in the first person. The words *I*, *me*, and *myself* are not part of the résumé.

❑ The résumé is written with *Times New Roman or Arial style font in 11- or 12-point* size. It should be printed on simple white, cream, or gray paper. No colors, pastels, or special textures other than résumé bond or plain copy paper should be used.

❑ The résumé is one to two pages, never more than two pages. (The exception to this is if you have a large number of scientific publications and/or patents. In that case, submit them as addendum on a separate sheet of paper, after asking whether or not the hiring authority wants to see them.)

## Radical Career Changes

If you're making a drastic career change—say, from attorney to fashion designer—I recommend that you still use the same format as above, but you should make some important alterations in the summary statement section of your résumé.

Unless you are using the tactic of Just Dive In!, it is likely that to hasten your transition, you've enrolled in a strategic education course, have started or even completed a certification program in your new field, and/or had the benefit of an internship or volunteer position.

Since we already know that employers are likely to get only a three- to seven-second "snapshot" of the first few lines of your résumé, it's imperative that you build strategies like internship, short-term education, and strategic education right into the summary statement at the beginning of the résumé so that they will see that you're already a "player" in their game.

Things that place you on the same playing field are experience (even if it's only in an academic or volunteer setting); specific statements about some areas in which you have concrete, immediately usable skills; or personal qualities that would reflect favorably on

Marie L. Sanchez
757 North Elmwood Drive
Los Gatos, CA 95136
(408) 337-2481 Work      (408) 297-3373 Home
(831) 223-9798 Mobile
marie_s@techmail.com

## Objective
A position as an environmental planner

## Summary
Over 10 years' experience as a landscaper and landscape designer as the owner of Big Bear Landscapes, specializing in native plants, low maintenance gardens, and waterfall design. Responsible for landscaping a 12-acre property with low-maintenance native plants, coming in eight days under deadline and $1,300 under budget. BS biology, Yale University. Currently enrolled in a course of study leading to a master's degree in environmental planning at California State University at Burlingame. Flexible, dependable, adaptable to change.

## Employment History
Big Bear Landscapes, Saratoga, CA 1993–present
Owner

- Designed and implemented a plan for a 13-acre residential property in Los Altos, California, using low-maintenance native California plants which was photographed and printed in *Better Homes and Landscapes* magazine.

- Saved a total of $1,300 by completing work eight days before deadline on a commercial property in San Jose, California.

- Reduced water usage and water bills by an average of 35 percent on each of 23 residential properties.

*Sample Résumé*

- Invited to lecture 60 community college students on the topic of native plant maintenance for the horticulture department at Hillsdale Community College in Fremont, California.
- Expert in native plants and plant biology. Able to identify over 300 varieties of native plants and succulents of the coastal region of the western United States.
- Trained and supervised a crew of 17 employees.

Anderson's Nursery, Los Gatos, CA  1989–1993
Outdoor Products Manager  (1991–1993)

- Sold approximately $450 worth of merchandise daily to up to 120 customers per week.
- Hired, trained, and managed 11 employees.
- Wrote a 28-page new employee orientation booklet.
- Recommended soil treatments, gardening methods, and gardening tools to customers.

Outdoor Gardening Associate  1989–1991

- Served up to 30 customers daily.
- Counseled customer on proper plant selection and garden care.
- Operated a cash register and credit card processor.
- Won Employee of the Month awards in January 1990 and September 1993.

### Education
Currently enrolled in graduate studies in environmental planning, California State University at Burlingame
BS in biology, with honors, Yale University, New Haven, Connecticut

*Sample Résumé (Continued)*

you in your new profession (dependability, ability to work under pressure, friendliness, ability to meet deadlines, and so on).

Finally, it's always a great idea to join some sort of professional organization that represents your field. As a participant (even passively) in the organization, you will seem to be that much more a member of a new team of professionals.

The best way to find organizations to which your new colleagues belong is to either search for them online—try, for example, *financial association, finance professional organizations,* or *financial planning networks*—or go to the library and look through a copy of the *Encyclopedia of Associations.*

You may be surprised at how many professional organizations exist for just about every occupation that exists. These groups may charge annual or monthly dues starting at as little as $5 a month and running as high as $600 a year. You should consider joining one or several. It would be money well spent.

Remember: Half the battle in getting hired is not *what* you know but how the employer perceives what you know. "Packaging" yourself as part of a professional or trade association can add as much credibility to your presentation as could years of schooling and experience.

## Summary Statements for Radical Career Changers

If you were making a radical career change from an engineer to a financial planner, it would do little good to lead your summary statement with "10 years as an engineer." Instead, it would be better (assuming you had completed some financial courses) to lead with something like this:

> Knowledge of state insurance practices and 401k and Keogh plans. Expertise in mathematics due to a master's degree in engineering and 10 years as an engineer. Effective interpersonal skills gained from 7 years managing over 18 people as a project manager. Professional, meticulous, responsible. Currently enrolled in a course of study leading to a certificate in financial planning at the University of Michigan extension. Member, Michigan Institute for the Development of Financial Advisement.

Similarly, one way our administrative assistant's summary statement could instantly downplay her years of serving as a secretary and highlight her midwifery training—however brief—could be something like this:

Experienced in midwifery assistance and prenatal and postnatal care. Excellent grasp of massage techniques, basic herbology, and interpersonal relations. Graduate of a certification course in midwifery assistance. Experienced in assisting in breach and other difficult birthing scenarios. Trustworthy, warm, empathetic. Member of Midwife Society of America.

## How to Submit Your Résumé

The *ideal* way to submit your résumé is to place a "warm" or "cold" phone call to the decision maker (something we'll discuss in the section of this chapter called "How to Make Direct Contact with a Decision Maker"). Second best would be an in-person interview, at which you present your résumé directly to the employer at the time of the interview.

When neither of those routes is possible, I'd like you to *beat your competition* by using an alternative to the regular U.S. mail service.

---

**Whether you are penetrating the unadvertised job market or responding to the advertised job market, sending your résumé by normal U.S. mail is the least effective way to get it noticed.**

---

Hiring managers are flooded with e-mail, which means that although an e-mail message is fast—almost instantaneous—your résumé will not receive the attention it deserves if you are up against up to 300 other e-mails per day.

To sway the odds back in your favor, use one of these methods:

1. Send it via Federal Express (FedEx).
2. Send it through the U.S. Postal Service Priority Mail in a Priority Mail envelope.
3. Fax it.

---

**There is no mail that is opened faster than an overnight FedEx package slated for arrival by 10 a.m. the next morning.**

---

Both the color of the FedEx envelope and the urgency conveyed by overnight delivery create an almost *irresistible* urge for the receiver to see what's inside. FedEx can be a little expensive though. USPS Priority Mail, also because of its red and blue motif and its priority status, quickly captures the interest of its recipient.

## Submitting a Résumé on the Internet

If you plan to submit a résumé using the Internet, *be careful* not to fall into the trap of clicking on the "apply here" or "apply now" button (usually located at the bottom of the page on your computer screen).

Because this is the easiest way to apply, hundreds and even thousands of others will be doing the same thing. Instead, we have found that faxing your resume to the fax number on the online advertisement is the superior way to get it noticed. You also have the option of sending it by FedEx or USPS Priority Mail.

## Cover Letter or No Cover Letter?

I've spoken to hundreds of people with the power to hire others. The vast majority of these people have so little time to even read your résumé that they consider a cover letter to be just so much more paper to "wade" through. I don't recommend that you write a cover letter unless it is *explicitly* asked for. If you happen to need a cover letter because you've spotted a written request for it, please see the following sample approach cover letter to use as your guide.

# Q Letters

A *Q letter* (or *qualifications letter*) is a special kind of cover letter, and I highly recommend its use. It can be submitted *with or without* a résumé. Using the same type of quantifiable statements you created for your résumé, a Q letter gives the employer a swift and efficient glance at how your qualifications stack up to the requirements of the job.

Q letters have been amazingly effective for people who have used them. You will see in the following sample Q cover letter that they certainly meet our "seven-second first look" requirements.

They're an attention getter, they communicate relevant data in a concise format, and hiring managers report that they like them.

July 15, 20xx


Dr. Paul Robinson
125 Doctor Lane
Madison, WI 12345

Dear Dr. Robinson:

Hello. I am interested in the position of midwife assistant in your clinic, either at present or some time in the future. I possess the following qualifications:

- Graduate of the Doula program at West Denver Institute of Midwifery.
- Successful internship, which included assisting in 12 births at the Gentle Birth Center.
- Knowledge of prenatal, birthing, and postpartum procedures for labor assistants.
- Excellent interpersonal skills due to three years volunteering at Colorado Mountains Hospice Program.
- Three letters of recommendation.

Please expect a call from me within three business days, after you have had an opportunity to review my qualifications.

Sincerely,


Alice Livermore
(727) 333-6760
livermorea@cbc.net

*Sample Approach Letter or Cover Letter*

Ethan Jenner
1659 7th Avenue
Heraldtown, Vermont
(416) 555-5555
ejenner@emailaddress.com

February 22, 20xx

Ms. Deborah Scott
ABC Corporation
23 Broadway
Washington, DC 12345

Dear Ms. Scott:

In response to your advertisement for a chief financial officer in the Monday, February 21, 20xx, posting on www.monster.com, I would like to respectfully submit my qualifications.

| Your Requirements | My Qualifications |
|---|---|
| 1. Five to 10 years' experience as a CFO in a Fortune 500 company. | Over 10 years' experience as a CFO. |
| 2. Oversees other accountants. | Supervised more than 12 accountants and high-level financial personnel. |
| 3. CPA desired. | CPA since 1985. |
| 4. BA required, MBA preferred. | BA in history. Currently enrolled in a course of study leading to an MBA from the University of Vermont. |

Please call me at your earliest convenience for an interview. Thank you.

Sincerely,

Ethan Jenner

*Sample Q Letter or Cover Letter*

## *Compose Your Own Q Letter*

The way to write a Q letter is to first determine the requirements of the job. You can do this by looking at a job description, looking at a general description in the O*NET, or by asking a person already in that profession what the typical requirements are.

Then, pick four or five requirements and write them on the left half of your page (see sample). On the right side of your page, for every requirement find a qualification you possess that is equal to or better than the requirement.

# How to Make Direct Contact with a Decision Maker

Once you've sent your résumé and Q letter, it's time to make direct contact. So, just what does *direct contact* mean? Direct contact means placing a "warm" or "cold" telephone call to a key decision maker in a company for which you want to work. On the phone, you convince him or her to set up a face-to-face meeting with you.

By *warm call* I mean a call that is preceded by some sort of written communication—a letter, a résumé, or note of some kind. See the earlier samples of an approach letter and Q letter and the following warm-call pitch:

> Hello, Dr. Thomas. My name is Alice Livermore. I'm a midwife assistant graduate of West Denver Institute of Midwifery and an intern from the Gentle Birth Center. *You may have noticed from the FedEx I sent you* that I have excellent references and a good grasp of the birthing process. When can I come in for an interview?

A *cold call* is made directly to your contact, without any written introduction, such as the following example:

> Hello, Dr. Thomas. My name is Alice Livermore. I'm a midwife assistant graduate of West Denver Institute of Midwifery and an intern from the Gentle Birth Center. I have excellent references and a good grasp of the birthing process. When can I come in for an interview?

Both cold and warm calls work (although a cold call has the element of a "surprise attack" that can be quite effective). A cold call, we have found, can actually be more effective when placing a call to executives, upper managers, and business owners because the very methods you are using to place the call—aggressiveness, proactivity, courage, initiative—are sometimes the very qualities that brought the executive up "out of the ranks" and the very ones he or she will most admire in you. It's up to you which kind of calling best suits your personality and the particular situation.

## Four Steps for Making Direct Contact

Remembering what you know now about the unadvertised job market, these four steps are the game plan for getting yourself an interview:

1. Choose up to 40 companies or businesses for which you'd like to work, regardless of whether or not they have an advertised job opening. You can generate your list from the business directory of the phone book, from hoovers.com on the Internet, or from *Rich's Guide, Standard & Poor's Directory, Reference USA,* or *Thomas Register,* which are available in hard copy (and sometimes online) at your local library.

2. Determine the *exact first and last name* of the person most likely to have the power to hire you. Most often, this is the person who is the boss of *your* next potential boss.

   So if you are a manager, rather than calling a senior manager, you would call the *director* or vice president. Similarly, if you were a director you would call the executive vice president or the chief operating officer. If you are calling a small company, ask for the owner or manager.

   You can find exact names of managers and executives on the Web site of the company or, in one of the *directories listed above in step 1.* Or you may have to use a direct approach.

   For a direct approach, call the receptionist of the business and say, "I'm going to send a FedEx to the *(vice president, manager, director)* of *(marketing, engineering, manufacturing, health services, production).* Can you give me the exact spelling of his or her name?" Three times out of five, you'll get the name.

3. Send a fax, USPS Priority Mail, or FedEx with your Q letter or approach letter (see sample on page 144). You may send the letter alone or with a résumé. The approach letter is a great way to strike up productive communication with someone

you've never met before. This, or a Q letter, sent with or without a résumé, is excellent for laying the groundwork for a warm call.

4. Place a call to the person one to three days after the expected arrival of the letter. See the next section for details on what to say during your call.

---

> ***The procedure for a cold call is the same as the preceding four steps except that you do not precede the call with a letter or any form of written communication. In other words, skip step 3.***

---

## *Your 30-Second Phone Pitch*

The core of your cold or warm call is something that is sometimes referred to as a *30-second pitch*. You can compose your own pitch by using portions of the summary statement from your résumé. Let's take a moment to rehearse this technique so that you can get the feel of writing your own pitch. Take a look at the previous samples of both a warm- and a cold-call phone pitch. Use the following phone pitch template to construct your own pitch for a cold call or a warm call. You will have to make slight modifications in this pitch template to suit your own situation. Just keep in mind that your pitch has a very specific aim.

---

Hello, my name is _____. I have _____ years' experience as a _____, and I'm currently making a career change into the field of _____. I have an (AA, MA, etc.) degree in _____, and I just finished a certificate program in _____. (Optional) You may have noticed in my letter to you that _____. When can I come in for an interview?

---

*Cold- or Warm-Call Pitch Template*

The purpose of the pitch (for both a warm and a cold call) is to accomplish the following:

- Grab the listener's attention.
- Impress him or her with one or more of your qualifications.
- Target your statement to those qualifications you think the employer values most.
- If possible, mention a relevant fact you have learned to prove that you have researched the company.
- Ask for an interview. (An interview is *any* face-to-face contact with the employer.)

## Handling Screening-Out Questions and Objections

It's rather unlikely that the decision maker is going to answer the phone initially. It's more likely that you'll get a receptionist, supervisor, or executive assistant whose job it is to screen out unwanted calls. In large companies there may even be more than one of these assistants.

The script in the section "Making the Phone Call" will show you exactly what those assistants are trained to say—and you may be pleasantly surprised that the dialogue shows you exactly how to counter their screening efforts and get past them to the hiring manager.

You'll also notice that it's unlikely (though not at all impossible) that the decision maker will agree to a meeting the first time you ask. The sample phone script shows you exactly what we've found to be the typical doubts (we call them *objections*) that the employer may have.

Again, it may surprise you when you actually start making calls that, indeed, these are exactly the objections you encounter. Fortunately, you'll be prepared. Before you make a call, be careful that you are comfortable with your pitch and know the tactics for getting past the assistants. Also, learn to anticipate the objections the employer will raise and become competent at dealing with them.

## Making the Phone Call

When three business days have passed since you sent your letter to the decision maker, it's time for you to give him or her a phone call. At this juncture, it's a good idea to practice your phone script with a friend or family member several times before you go for the real thing. If you feel a bit jittery about ringing up your No. 1 favorite company, try a "dry run" with a few companies (even companies out of town) that you don't care too much about.

With a little practice you'll get into the rhythm of getting through the screening process with the receptionist and countering typical objections from the employer. With your phone script in hand, this should be a breeze! The following is a script of a typical warm call.

---

### Phone rings

RECEPTIONIST: Hello, Ellen Robinson Childbirth Clinic.

JOB SEEKER: Alice Livermore for Dr. Robinson.

RECEPTIONIST: May I ask the nature of your call? *(Screening out—see below.)*

JOB SEEKER: It's business.

RECEPTIONIST: All right, I'll connect you.

DOCTOR'S ASSISTANT: Maya Rhodes speaking.

JOB SEEKER: Alice Livermore for Dr. Robinson.

DOCTOR'S ASSISTANT: This is Dr. Robinson's nurse. Can I help you? *(Screening out.)*

JOB SEEKER: No, but thank you. I'd prefer to speak to Dr. Robinson directly.

DOCTOR'S ASSISTANT: What is this regarding? *(Screening out.)*

JOB SEEKER: It's about a document I FedExed to her yesterday.

DOCTOR'S ASSISTANT: Is she expecting your call? *(Screening out.)*

JOB SEEKER: Yes. *(Remember, you faxed or sent something saying you would call.)*

DOCTOR'S ASSISTANT: All right, I'll connect you.

---

*Sample Phone Script*

HIRING MANAGER: Dr. Robinson.

JOB SEEKER: (*This paragraph is what is referred to as the pitch.*) Hello, Dr. Robinson. My name is Alice Livermore. I'm a mid-wife assistant graduate of West Denver Institute of Midwifery. I had a 30-day internship and participated in 12 births at the Gentle Birth Center. You may have noticed *from the FedEx I sent you* that I have excellent references and a good grasp of the birthing process. When can I come in for an interview?

HIRING MANAGER: Did I get your FedEx? Oh, yes, let me see . . . It's right here on my desk. Hmm . . . Yes, Alice it does look like you have some excellent skills. Unfortunately, we're not hiring right now. (*Objection.*)

JOB SEEKER: Oh, that's fine. I'm not interested in just *any* company, and I *don't need a job right away.* I'm looking for an organization that's a good match for my skills so that I can make a long-term commitment. (*Optional: I looked at your Web site, and I really like your clinic's philosophy on child bearing, especially the quote by Margaret Mead.*) I'm interested in talking to you about *future* or *unexpected* openings.

HIRING MANAGER: Can you send me your full résumé? (*This is an objection, a way to keep you at bay, not an invitation to an interview. It would be easy for the employer to simply toss your résumé into the "read-later" pile or even in the paper shredder. A living, breathing person with whom you're interacting face to face is much more of an investment than handling a piece of paper. You want the employer to invest in meeting you in the flesh.*)

JOB SEEKER: Of course, thank you, but I will be in your area of town next week. I'd love to schedule a very brief 15-minute talk and get your *personal opinion* on my qualifications.

HIRING MANAGER: Well, . . . I'd like to but I'm just jammed with patients next week. (*Objection.*)

JOB SEEKER: No problem at all. How about if we schedule something for the following week, say, Wednesday or Thursday? How would that work for you?

*Sample Phone Script (Continued)*

HIRING MANAGER: Actually, on that week, Friday the 22nd would probably be better.

JOB SEEKER: Morning or afternoon?

HIRING MANAGER: Let's see. My morning is booked.

JOB SEEKER: Would 2 p.m. or 3 p.m. work?

HIRING MANAGER: Yes, why don't I see you at 3. I'll transfer you back to the receptionist, and she'll make the appointment for you.

JOB SEEKER: Thanks so much, Dr. Robinson, I'm looking forward to it!

HIRING MANAGER: Goodbye.

JOB SEEKER: See you on the 22nd.

*Sample Phone Script (Continued)*

## Perseverance Pays!

It's certainly *possible* that you will *not* have to deal at all with being screened or with the employer's having objections. I know someone who made a cold call to a medium-sized company on a holiday. Guess who answered? The president of the company. Who else would be there on a holiday? The president was so impressed with the bravado of the caller's phone pitch that *he offered her a job on the spot*—on the phone!

> **If you get the decision maker's voice mail, it is best not to leave a message. That puts the ball in his or her court. Try the phone call later.**

Perseverance really pays off when it comes to warm and cold calling. One of my clients to whom I taught direct-contact techniques called me after the second call and said she couldn't do it. I urged her to continue. She called me after her eleventh call and said she'd absolutely had it.

After talking for a while, she decided to give it one more try. Her twelfth call, to Time Warner, yielded a talk with a vice president. He granted her an interview. She now has a job, earning over $100,000 a year.

Is an hour of making repeated phone calls, and possibly facing momentary rejection, worth that kind of money? You decide! Your goal is not to sound polished or even friendly. *Your goal is to get an interview.*

Once you get the interview, stand up and cheer! Then, send the hiring manager a brief note or e-mail confirming the date and time of the meeting and thanking him or her in advance for his or her time. (See the following sample confirmation letter.)

## Preparing for the Interview

You made it! Now it's time to prepare for your interview. One of the very best ways to prepare is to know your talents and skills and be ready to tell anecdotes (examples) about how and when you used those talents. Preferably your specific examples should be in story form using quite *specific* details and *Q statements*.

Since you are a career changer and you don't yet have stories to tell about your new career, you may have to bring your *transferable talents* from former occupations, school, or even hobbies to bear in your interview.

### Transferable Talents

Remember, transferable talents are things like analysis, management, and problem-solving and interpersonal skills that can transfer from one occupation to a completely different one. Here is a list of transferable talents, similar to the list we saw in Chapter 2. Check off each of these skills you have performed—you need not be an expert. You may need to rely on talents you haven't used since high school, but if you used them once, you can improve upon them and use them again!

❑ Advertising      ❑ Arranging

❑ Advising      ❑ Assessing performance

❑ Analyzing      ❑ Assessing progress

November 2, 20xx

Robert Coleman
XYZ Big Company
789 First Street
Kansas City, MO 12345

Dear Mr. Coleman:

Thank you for your time on the telephone earlier today. I'm very pleased that we could set up a time for a meeting.

I know from my research that your company is well regarded for giving generously to charitable causes, and with two new offices opening in West Virginia this year, you must be enjoying great success.

I'm eager to meet you and find out more about XYZ Big Company. I'll look forward to our meeting at 9:30 a.m. on Thursday, December 2.

Thank you again.

Regards,


Amy Levin
(222) 756-9123 home
(222) 333-3433 mobile
alevin@fastnet.com

*Sample Letter of Confirmation*

- ❑ Assessing quality
- ❑ Assisting
- ❑ Attention to detail
- ❑ Auditing
- ❑ Budgeting
- ❑ Building cooperation
- ❑ Building credibility
- ❑ Building relation-
  ships
- ❑ Building structures
- ❑ Calculating
- ❑ Classifying
- ❑ Client relations
- ❑ Coaching
- ❑ Communicating
  feelings
- ❑ Communicating
  ideas
- ❑ Communicating in
  writing
- ❑ Communicating
  instructions
- ❑ Communicating
  nonverbally
- ❑ Communicating
  verbally
- ❑ Computer literate
- ❑ Conceptualizing
- ❑ Consulting
- ❑ Correcting
- ❑ Corresponding
- ❑ Counseling
- ❑ Customer service
- ❑ Data analysis

- ❑ Data processing
- ❑ Decision making
- ❑ Decorating
- ❑ Delegating
- ❑ Developing designs
- ❑ Developing systems
- ❑ Developing talent
- ❑ Diagnosing
- ❑ Directing
- ❑ Drafting
- ❑ Drawing
- ❑ Driving
- ❑ Editing
- ❑ Educating
- ❑ Empathizing
- ❑ Enforcing
- ❑ Engineering
- ❑ Evaluating
- ❑ Filing
- ❑ Financial
  planning
- ❑ Forecasting
- ❑ Formulating
- ❑ Fund raising
- ❑ Healing
- ❑ Helping others
- ❑ Imagining
- ❑ Implementing
- ❑ Influencing
- ❑ Initiating
- ❑ Intervening
- ❑ Intuiting
- ❑ Inventing

- ❏ Investigating
- ❏ Leading people
- ❏ Lecturing
- ❏ Lifting
- ❏ Listening
- ❏ Managing tasks
- ❏ Marketing
- ❏ Marketing and communications
- ❏ Massaging
- ❏ Nurturing
- ❏ Observing
- ❏ Organizing
- ❏ Prescribing
- ❏ Program managing
- ❏ Programming computers
- ❏ Project managing
- ❏ Promoting
- ❏ Public speaking
- ❏ Reconstructing
- ❏ Recording
- ❏ Repairing
- ❏ Reporting
- ❏ Researching
- ❏ Sales and marketing programs
- ❏ Selling
- ❏ Servicing
- ❏ Servicing customers
- ❏ Supervising
- ❏ Surveying
- ❏ Team building
- ❏ Team leading
- ❏ Telephone skills
- ❏ Tending
- ❏ Tooling
- ❏ Training
- ❏ Troubleshooting
- ❏ Understanding
- ❏ Using of equipment
- ❏ Using of the Internet

Now that you've completed the exercise, I'd like you to pick six of the talents you checked that you think you will most need in your future career.

1. _____
2. _____
3. _____
4. _____
5. _____
6. _____

For each of the talents that you picked, please write three quick stories about how, where, and when you used them, including the positive *results* of your efforts. Your interviewer will want to hear these stories as proof that you can really do what you claim you can do. You will shine as someone who is thoroughly prepared and knows his or her strengths.

---

**In a national study conducted by an organization called JIST in Indianapolis, 4,000 employers, declared that 85 percent of job candidates do not clearly state their strengths. You'll be in the top 15 percent by clarifying your talents and strengths and providing information to back them up.**

---

Use Q statements wherever you can, and be as detailed and specific as possible without going over about 90 seconds. Please write your stories (or keywords that help you remember them) in the following section. It's a good idea to have at least two stories for each talent you've selected. The *more* anecdotes you can relate, though, the more prepared you will feel and the more convincing you will be.

1. _____

    a. _____

    _____

    b. _____

    _____

    c. _____

    _____

2. _____

    a. _____

    _____

    b. _____

    _____

c. _____

_____

3. _____

   a. _____

_____

   b. _____

_____

   c. _____

_____

4. _____

   a. _____

_____

   b. _____

_____

   c. _____

_____

5. _____

   a. _____

_____

   b. _____

_____

   c. _____

_____

6. _____

   a. _____

_____

   b. _____

_____

c. _____

_____

Other _____

_____

## The Career Change Question

As a career changer you will most definitely be asked the following question during your interview: Why did you quit your former career?

The most favorable answer to this question is one that is *not* negative and does *not* reflect badly on you. An answer that indicates you were bored, "burned out," hated your old profession, had trouble with your boss or coworkers, were fired, or that you are seeking out a new career "just for the money" may sound negative or even petty to the interviewer.

Better answers to this question would be the following:

1. My last career was not a perfect match for my interests and skills. After researching this (*the new*) profession, I think I'm very well matched and would be very happy to be part of it.

2. I have been researching the profession of _____ (*the new career*), and I find it fascinating. There are some trends and innovations that really interest me, such as _____, and I'd like to make a career of being a _____.

> **Notice that the better answers to this question focus less on the old job and much more on the new career.**

## Other Typical Interview Questions

The following are some of the most common interview questions. Write your answer under each question, remembering to be specific and to not state anything bad about yourself, your former boss, or your former company. Emphasize your transferable skills with the specific *anecdotes* about your previous experiences you've just written.

Tell me about yourself.

_____

_____

What are some of your skills?

_____

_____

What are some of your most important accomplishments?

_____

_____

What are some of your personal strengths? Can you give me some examples?

_____

_____

What would your last boss (or coworkers) say about you?

_____

_____

What do you know about our company?

_____

_____

Why do you want to work with this company?

_____

_____

Why did you leave your last company?

_____

_____

Where do you see yourself in five years?

_____

_____

Are you better working independently or being part of a team?

_____

_____

What would you do if you found out one of your coworkers was stealing from the company?

_____

_____

How much were you making in your last job?

_____

What are your salary expectations at this company?

_____

_____

Why should I hire you?

_____

_____

Good! Now that you have at least two stories for each of your transferable talents, you can anticipate some of the most common questions, and you know how to answer the question "Why are you switching occupations?" then you're ready to shine during the interview. You can now go into the interview and be *fearless*.

## Follow-Up Letters

A letter following an interview should always be sent within 24 hours—mail or e-mail is fine. I call a thank-you note a *focus letter* because in a thank-you note you can further influence the employer by showing that you heard and thought about some of the items discussed at the interview.

You can also illustrate how your talents can help solve some of the problems or meet some of the goals of the company that you learned about during the meeting, such as tidbits about the interviewer (a golfer, bowler, swimmer, tennis player, pianist, a rock and roll fan), new product launches, new projects, company milestones, the interviewer's career path to management, same alma mater, anything else in common? Whatever indicates that you were an attentive listener can be important to allude to in the focus letter. Additionally, you can tactfully add anything valuable about yourself that you might have forgotten at the interview. (See the sample letter below.)

---

July 29, 20xx

Ms. Bettina Simmons
Executive Vice President
Ionit, Incorporated
554½ Second Avenue, Suite 237A
New York, NY 103xx

Dear Ms. Simmons:

What a pleasure it was to meet you earlier today! I must say I was very flattered that you extended our meeting from the half-hour we had planned to almost 90 minutes. I certainly appreciate your generosity in sharing your ideas about the company and acquainting me with Bob Delts and the others on the team.

Something in our exchange rang a bell for me, and I just thought I'd share it with you. You mentioned that Ionit would be opening an office soon in Minneapolis and that a senior vice president would be needed there for a time to get the January product launch off to a roaring start.

---

*Sample Letter to Follow an Interview*

I didn't mention it at the interview, but I happen to have experience with the marketing of D-Trek 5001 type software. I planned and executed a similar launch in my prior position at 4Tell, and I ended up saving the company almost a quarter of a million dollars by incorporating a direct-mailing component into the project.

I believe that I have the wisdom gained from experience to be instrumental in the same kinds of substantial savings for Ionit, and, if hired, I plan to present several scenarios that I think would be beneficial for the Minneapolis effort. I also am free to relocate there until the product is off to a healthy introduction.

Again, thank you for your time in the interview. If you have any questions I can answer or if you would like to see a sample proposal for my idea on the Minneapolis project, I would be happy to oblige.

Regards,


Han Nguyen
(212) 883-xxxx
h_nguyenvp@juno.com

*Sample Letter to Follow an Interview (Continued)*

*Every* time you send a piece of written communication to a hiring manager, follow it up within one to three days of its expected arrival with a phone call. Conversely, *every* time you talk to a hiring manager by phone, follow it up with a quick letter or e-mail.

This letter-phone-letter approach has been proven to work (as long as you have permission from the hiring manager to keep checking back every several days). By keeping your application at the forefront of the decision maker's mind, you are the first one she or he thinks of when an opening occurs.

Those of you who are planning on becoming entrepreneurs will most likely not need a résumé *or* an interview. Instead, you'll be in charge! The next chapter will get you started on your path to starting your own business.

CHAPTER NINE

# For Entrepreneurial Spirits

## Are You an Entrepreneur?

Although 80 percent of people in America say that they have thought about running their own business, thinking about it and actually doing it are two very different things. You may indeed have had some fears about choosing another profession and becoming part of a preexisting organization, but you may find that your uncertainties increase when you think about going out all on your own.

The best ways to fend off those kinds of fears are with facts—facts that you assess for yourself and objective data about the nature of being a business owner. Those facts are exactly the ones we'll examine in this chapter.

There are decidedly many good reasons to run your own business or become a consultant, but for every plus, there is also a minus. Anyone who owns his or her own business or consulting practice will tell you that there are both assets and liabilities in being your own boss.

The purpose of this chapter is not to tell you how to set up and run your own enterprise. That would be the subject of a whole book! Rather, it is to assist you in figuring out the important question of whether or not you want to take on the responsibilities of being an entrepreneur or independent consultant and to point out to you the best resources you can access for free to answer all the questions you have about starting your own company or consultancy.

# Pros and Cons of Starting Your Own Business

If you feel strongly that owning your own business or being a consultant is your authentic calling, then *nothing else*—not a personality or an aptitude test, not a friend or family member, not a banker or financial advisor, not a career counselor, maybe not even your own spouse or significant other—will be able to stop you.

That's good because even if you have all the support the world can offer, *you will still be challenged repeatedly* to demonstrate a deep desire to succeed under just about any circumstance if your business is to survive and thrive.

> **Yes, there are pros and cons, but your own gut feeling—your own thoughtful analysis—is what must guide you in making this important choice.**

The lists below show some of the advantages and disadvantages of owning your own business. Read them carefully and begin to formulate your own ideas about your entrepreneurial fitness.

**Possible Advantages**

- You are in charge.

- You create your own schedule. When you're more established, you may be able to work fewer and/or more flexible hours. You may even be able to work from home.

**Possible Disadvantages**

- You must assume 100% responsibility for both successes and failures. This does not necessarily mean *personal* legal responsibility if you choose a corporation as a business structure.

- You may work up to 100 hours per week getting started. You are basically "on call" all the time until you hire someone else to help you or you "automate" your business to run itself.

| Possible Advantages | Possible Disadvantages |
|---|---|
| • Your income is limited only by your ability to make a profit for yourself. | • Your income may differ considerably from month to month and year to year. |
| • You can choose with whom you want to work. | • Employees and even business partners can present problems such as cheating, lack of motivation, or legal or disciplinary issues. (You can hire an on-call human resources consultant to help you with employee issues.) |
| • You have almost unlimited creativity. | • People with money to loan you may not agree with your creative ideas. You must persevere to find funding or fund your business yourself. |
| • You can choose the image you wish to portray to the public. | • Some advertising, marketing, and public relations efforts can be expensive. You may need to market yourself constantly to stay competitive. |
| • Most small businesses, consultants, and corporations enjoy considerable tax benefits. | • None. |

Consider carefully whether the advantages are *attractive* enough for you to take some major risks along the way in order to achieve your desired result. Also note whether or not you think you can *persevere* in the face of some of the disadvantageous aspects of running your own enterprise or being a private consultant.

# Self-Assessment

The following pages present a test, or *self-assessment,* to help you think about some of the skills and personality traits that might be beneficial to you while you face the ups and downs of entrepreneurship or consultancy.

> ***The test results should be construed not as the
> final answer as to whether you should make
> the choice to own your own business, but
> rather as a tool to show you the strengths
> you already possess and the areas you may want
> to improve on. It's up to you to assess the
> results, and it's up to you to decide whether own-
> ing your own business is really right for you at
> this time in your life.***

Remember, both the self-assessment and the chart are not meant to be scientifically conclusive in any way but are instead tools for research and self-awareness. The assessment is best used if you put it into action.

For example, if you find that you have several areas that need improvement, you can learn them from a book, a correspondence course, an online class, or perhaps a night class. You can even hire an executive coach to get you up to par on your leadership abilities and required skills.

Before we go any further, let's see how you match up to some of the classic traits, tasks, and obstacles inherent in the process of running a business or a private consulting practice.

Please answer the following questions by putting a check in the box to the left of the statement if the statement is true for you. You cannot "fail" the test, so take a moment to reflect and answer each question as accurately as possible.

- ❑  I'm a risk taker.
- ❑  I am very independent minded.
- ❑  I am results oriented.
- ❑  I consistently demand the best from myself.
- ❑  I am comfortable researching or asking others about things I don't know.
- ❑  I trust action more than analysis.
- ❑  I can overcome failure and recommit my energies to success.

- ❏ I am sometimes impatient for results.
- ❏ I am good at managing money.
- ❏ I plan and use my time carefully.
- ❏ Sometimes I'm a bit of a perfectionist.
- ❏ I consider myself a very hard worker.
- ❏ I am ambitious.
- ❏ I have a vision of how I want things to be, and I follow through until my vision is realized.
- ❏ I am a leader.
- ❏ I will do almost anything if it's ethical to attain my goals.
- ❏ I dislike being supervised.
- ❏ I dislike routine tasks.
- ❏ I am determined to win.
- ❏ I dislike being on someone else's timetable.
- ❏ The goals I set for myself are higher than average.
- ❏ I am confident.
- ❏ I am able to make on-the-spot decisions.
- ❏ I like myself.
- ❏ I am competitive.
- ❏ I have integrity.
- ❏ I do not need a salary; I prefer my earnings to be unlimited.
- ❏ I am willing to work up to 80 or 100 hours a week to get my business off the ground.
- ❏ I realize that I may have to "wear many hats"—even some that I don't like such as bookkeeper, marketing director, secretary, CEO, or receptionist—when my business first gets started.
- ❏ I see failure as a learning experience.
- ❏ I am good at persuading people to see my way.
- ❏ I'm a creative problem solver.
- ❏ I am not afraid to seek expert advice from others.
- ❏ Sometimes other people think I am very opinionated.
- ❏ I am comfortable with periods of uncertainty, including financial uncertainty.
- ❏ I believe in myself.

If you checked at least 50 percent (about 16) of the items on the above assessment, you probably have what it takes to own your own business or be a consultant *if and only if* you are *willing to grow* and seek help for the areas that need improvement.

If you got a lower score, it doesn't mean you can't be an entrepreneur. You might interpret a lower score as feedback that you have a couple of areas that will require extra focus.

Now, analyze what you've checked off. What areas do you think are your best assets? Which ones might need some extra attention?

- ❑ Self-confidence
- ❑ Risk taking
- ❑ Leadership
- ❑ Tolerance for uncertainty
- ❑ Tolerance for an uneven income
- ❑ Seeking out new knowledge and expert advice
- ❑ Motivation and ambition
- ❑ High self-esteem

If you're going to turn a weakness into a strength, you've got to commit it to writing and make a plan, just as you would do with any other goal. Either fill in the blanks below as a reminder to yourself or use one of the goal templates from Chapter 6 to note your plans. Either way, *develop a plan* and stick to it. If you find you're off course, adjust and try a new tactic or ask others for their feedback.

The one chief area of improvement that I will attack in the next month:

_____

_____

Here is my plan of attack:

_____

_____

Perhaps the first thing to think about when your business is in the planning phase is deciding what kind of business you want and what structure you want the business to have. Before you write a formal business plan, take a moment and think about the answers to the following questions:

1. Will you sell a product or service or both?

   _____

   _____

2. What kind of products will you sell?

   _____

   _____

3. What kind of service will you sell?

   _____

   _____

4. Why will your product or service be more attractive to customers or clients than what your competitors may provide?

   _____

   _____

5. Who will be your customers or clients? Ages? Gender? Financial status? Geographic area? Educational background? Special interests? Marital status?

   _____

   _____

6. What "problem" will your product or service solve for individuals, families, communities, and the environment? The world?

   _____

   _____

7. Will you start a business from scratch, build a consulting practice, buy an existing business, or own and operate a franchise?

   _____

   _____

8. Where, ideally, would the home base of your business be located? Office? Factory? Laboratory? Warehouse? Outdoors? Your home? On the Internet?

---

---

These informal questions will get you started in thinking about some of the basic components of your business plan, which I recommend that you write with the assistance of a class or mentor from the Small Business Administration (SBA), a government organization that offers free assistance to entrepreneurs.

## The U.S. Small Business Administration

Keeping all of these things in mind, your next step is to get in touch with the Small Business Administration (SBA) near you or go to its Web site, www.sba.gov, and begin to explore some of the state-of-the-art, *no-cost* offerings for entrepreneurs. Make an appointment with one of the mentors, and start writing a formal business plan.

> *The Small Business Administration is a nationwide network of U.S. government offices dedicated to helping budding entrepreneurs like you in all aspects of getting started in a successful venture.*

There are SBA offices, where you can have access to in-person classes and advisement, in most medium to large cities. If you would prefer to take advantage of online training via the Internet, that too is available. The SBA's information is absolutely invaluable, and it may be just as good as you would receive in a more expensive, privately run business program. The SBA also supplies easy access to small-business loans underwritten by the government and/or cooperating banks. Here are some of the seminars and services offered by the organization:

- Determining a legal structure for your business—sole proprietorship, partnership, limited liability corporation (LLC), S corporation, or C corporation.

- Buying an existing business or starting a franchise.

- All aspects of business funding—government funding, private-bank loans, credit considerations, angel investors, venture capital firms, self-generated funding, or equity funding.

- Financial management—bookkeeping for small businesses, financial forecasting, understanding financial statements, and accounting and taxation issues.

- Marketing and promotion—the latest, most efficient, and most cost-effective means to market, advertise, and promote your new business. In concert with the Small Business Development Centers www.sba.gov/sbdc/ (with links on the SBA Web site), they provide instruction on how to write a marketing plan for your business.

- Liaison to SCORE, a group of retired executives who have already had the experience of building and running one or more successful businesses (www.score.org). The SBA offers one-on-one mentorship to new entrepreneurs from people in the community who have already assembled successful companies.

## A Practice Business Plan

If you'd like to practice formulating a business plan, there is an excellent template for doing so on *Microsoft PowerPoint*, which is part of the *Microsoft Office* computer program. You can also find business plan templates at a very reasonable price at most computer software or office supply stores. To get to the *Microsoft PowerPoint template*, which guides you with written prompts all the way through a business plan and marketing plan:

1. Open the *PowerPoint* program.
2. Click on the choice marked Design Template.
3. Click on the Presentations tab.

4. Click on the Business Plan icon.

5. Later, if you'd also like to write a separate marketing plan, click on the Marketing Plan icon.

All the transferable-skills exercises you've done in previous chapters can be put to use here. There are many skills you may have developed over a lifetime in both work- and non-work-related settings that can be of value in starting your own business. Even if you've never been a CEO, you may have been captain of the volleyball team! You'll need essentially the same abilities for planning strategies, communicating effectively, and being at the helm of the ship when you're in your new office as when you were on the courts. If you've never managed a business or budget before, just think about what it takes to run a household or maintain a car—budgeting, cleaning, maintenance.

Many of the things you presently just take for granted will be the recipe you'll need for success when you're running your own business. It may be a little scary at first, but there is an interesting paradox about the emotion we call fear. When we experience fear in our bodies, we feel an elevated heartbeat, increased rate of breathing, and a rush of blood to our extremities. The emotion of excitement causes exactly the same reaction in our bodies as does fear. Have you ever considered that your fear may *actually* be excitement? I challenge you to consider this conundrum! Remember your first date? Was that fear, or was it excitement? A little of both perhaps? Welcome to the world of running your own business!

Being your own boss can be one of the most rewarding choices that you can make in a lifetime. If you are willing to take the challenge along with the rewards, the sky's the limit!

# CHAPTER TEN

# Loving Your New Career

Congratulations! You've applied the fearless career change strategies and you have started your new job or business. You've faced your fears and overcome them, or you've found a powerful motivation to move through them. You've set new goals, anticipated the obstacles, and made plans to get past them. You have some superfast methods for bringing mere fantasies to full fruition.

Work is no longer a domain dominated by fear; it is a playground on which to stretch your limbs, a blank slate on which to sketch a brand-new blueprint. Now that you're on your way, it's time to learn not just how to *keep* a job or get promotions but how to really *thrive* in your new position or profession.

---

**When you are truly expressing your special talents and living your "authentic calling," a job is not just a job. It's a mission, designated to fulfill a "higher purpose."**

---

*Indeed, answering* your authentic calling becomes a *mission,* a bold adventure and a testing ground for newfound courage. Your task now is *not* just to perform job duties or to prevent yourself from being fired or going bankrupt (although preventing either of those eventualities is a good place to start).

If, then, you *are* on a mission, what is it? Well, it is certainly something that transcends just a job title or the name of your new business. There are lots of people out there merely doing job duties and trying not to get fired.

---

> ***Living with the mantle of your authentic calling will mean that you transcend routine, prescribed "duties" and go beyond "playing it safe." It means thinking big.***

---

Why would you start your own business if you just hope to break even or make enough money to get by? Surely with the special talents you bring to your new career or business you can hope for and even *demand* much more.

Again, what is *your* mission? It could be making a million dollars or hundreds of millions of dollars. It's been done before, and someone, somewhere will do it again. Your mission could be to become the finest and the best-known practitioner in your field. It may be to produce the most modern, efficient technology of its kind. Your mission could well be to relieve the world of suffering by making it a safer, more beautiful, more prosperous and peaceful place to live.

In Chapter 4, I briefly mentioned a woman who started a group focused on women's financial issues who charged $10 per person for a six-week program. At the time, she didn't know that disseminating her ideas was her authentic calling, but look what happened: She *started small* and *followed a path that beckoned to her*. Now, she has multiple best-selling books, has appeared on national television, is enjoying a syndicated magazine column, and earns large profits from the seminars she teaches.

What started as a job in which she was essentially earning less than $1 per hour ultimately became her mission. Her special purpose was not seeking the approval of others, settling for security, or staying out of the line of fire. It was her mission to make the world a better place by helping women to control and maximize their financial lives.

Her mission put her work into a much *larger* context than that of just making another dollar (although, as a result of following her calling, she is now a wealthy woman).

# Sample Mission Statement

In the seminars I teach, participants write their own mission statements. I'd like you to do the same, because no job is perfect all of the time. You are sure to have ups and downs in your career, but when you've committed to a mission—to something greater than any one of the individual tasks you perform daily—even unpleasant tasks seem worthwhile. You'll be reminded, by recalling your mission, that even the darkest of times cannot endure when your higher purpose is guiding your efforts.

> *Writing your mission statement may very well be the most important fearless career change exercise, one that will shape the long-term character of both your career and your life.*

Here are some examples of mission statements:

1. To provide exceptional quality ergonomic devices and training by maintaining the highest manufacturing standards and teaching methods so that people at work will experience less stress, more ease, greater efficiency, and better health and will live longer, more productive lives.

2. To give back to the community by creating a corporation that sells discount goods and services on the Internet and contributes 30 percent of all profits to charities and community concerns so that customers get items and services at fair prices and needy, sick, undereducated, and disadvantaged people can lead more happy and successful lives.

3. To lead my company to be the No. 1 manufacturer of routers in the world by practicing the highest of human ethics and morals in all of my personal and business affairs so that all of my employees will experience a safe, secure, equitable, and harmonious workplace, and the company will make profits of over $200 million annually.

## *Your Own Mission Statement*

You may observe that the structure of the example mission statements is relatively similar. They all begin by answering the question, "What am I doing?" Then they move on to "How am I doing it?" And, finally, they ask, "Why am I doing it?"

It takes serious thought, focused concentration, and honest reflection on the most important aspects of work and our *most essential purpose* in life to write a meaningful mission statement that will actually *serve to guide* our actions and emotions. Using the three examples of the mission statements above, I would like you, carefully and respectfully, to compose your own credo.

People (and companies) with a mission are motivated within by a strong desire to succeed. They maintain a commitment to morals and ethical values, and they are less subject to flap with the winds of public opinion or transitory fads. Your mission statement helps to solidify your new vocation, to brand it not just with things you are "good" at doing but with things that are deeply and intrinsically good.

Your statement does not have to reflect that you want to save the whole world, although if you feel that's your authentic calling, that *is* what you should write. Your mission statement is about *you* and your *relationship* to the career and life you want.

It need be only two or three sentences, but it must serve the purpose of inspiring you to the apex of your abilities and encouraging you through difficult or fearful times. The statement you write today may very well evolve into something else tomorrow or a year from now. That's fine. A mission statement is a "living" thing. That means that it grows and transforms with time. Please write your own mission statement for today on the lines below:

_____

_____

_____

_____

_____

_____

By overcoming your fears and creating a better career for yourself, you've crafted a better life. When your life aligns with its true purpose, you can't help but make the world a better place and set an example for everyone you meet. Your new vocation may not be glamorous or even heroic. It may be very ordinary. Like the man who repairs shoes.

Every time I go to my shoemaker and he hands me my finished shoes, I notice his unmistakable pride in the work he has done. It is as if, by simply shining shoes, replacing heels, and fixing insoles, he is performing a work of art. He looks very happy to me. He is a man with a mission, and though I don't pretend to know what it is, it is palpable. This man does his work with a kind of integrity that is possible only when answering to an authentic calling. When I leave his store, I'm not just carrying a bag of shoes. His happiness goes with me.

# INDEX

# Index

Classified advertisements, 129–131
"Cold" telephone calls, 142
  described, 146–147
  making, 147–152
  perserverance and, 152–153
  purpose of, 149
  template for, 148
Community (two-year) colleges:
  short-term education and, 71
  strategic education and, 62–66,
    79–85
Compassion skills, 23–24
Confirmation letters, 153, 154
*Consultant's Guide to Publicity, The*
  (Franklin), 110
Cover letters:
  sample, 144
  use of, 143

Deadlines, in goal-setting, 119–120
Degree programs, 62–63, 81–85
Depression, and need for career
  change, 1
Design skills, 20–21, 27
Detail skills, 24
Direct contact, 99–100, 131–153
  "cold" telephone calls in, 142,
    146–152
  interviews in, 153–162
  making, 149–152
  objections in, 149, 150–152
  perserverance in, 152–153
  résumés and, 131–143
  screening-out questions in, 149,
    150–152
  steps for making, 147–148
  unadvertised job market and,
    128–131
  "warm" telephone calls in, 142,
    146–152
Directing skills, 25
Distance learning programs, 81–85
Dreams, and need for career change,
  1

E-mail, submitting résumés by, 142
Edison, Thomas, 5

Education (*see* Training and
  education)
Empathy skills, 23–24
Employment development
  department (EDD), 80–81
*Encyclopedia of Associations*, 141
Entrepreneurship, 77–78, 165–174
  combined with other strategies,
    111–113
  defined, 77
  as fast-track strategy, 77–78,
    111–113
  financial issues in, 110, 112,
    172–173
  nature of, 165
  opportunities with start-up
    companies, 131
  planning for, 170–172, 173–174
  pros and cons of, 166–167
  resources for, 112, 172–173
  self-assessment for, 167–172
  success stories based on, 111–113
Exhaustion, and need for career
  change, 1
Expert image, 110

Failure, fear of, 4–7
Fast-track strategies, 59–78
  combining, 78
  entrepreneurship, 77–78, 111–113
  internship, 67–70, 78, 106–107
  Just Dive In! method, 75–77
  on-the-job training, 66–67, 98–100
  short-term education, 70–73, 78,
    92–94, 100–103
  strategic education, 62–66, 78,
    79–85, 88–92, 103–106
  success stories based on, 87–116
  transferable skills/talents and,
    60–62, 108–111, 113–115
  volunteering, 74–75, 78, 95–97
Fax transmission, 142, 143, 147–148
Fears:
  about career change, 2–7
  of failure, 4–7
Federal Express (FedEx) deliveries,
  142–143, 147–148

## *About the Author*

**Marky Stein** (San Jose, California) is an internationally recognized career coach and author on the subjects of job interviewing and career transitioning. She frequently speaks at career conferences and is well known to readers of the *Wall Street Journal, USA Today,* the *Chicago Tribune,* the *Boston Globe,* the *Los Angeles Times,* and other major publications. Ms. Stein has worked as a career consultant to over 75 of the Fortune 500 companies. A regular guest on national television, radio, and Web casts, Ms. Stein is also recognized as the job search expert on Time Warner's popular Web site iVillage.com and the career transition expert for *Real Magazine.* She donates much of her time to teaching job search skills to homeless youth.